Ordinary Means, Extraordinary Ends

*Word, Sacrament,
and the Great Commission*

REFORMED FORUM

Copyright © 2025 Reformed Forum

Reformed Forum
1585 N. Milwaukee Ave.
Suite 113
Libertyville, IL 60048
www.reformedforum.org

All rights reserved. No part of this book may be used or reproduced in any manner whatsoever without written permission except in the case of brief quotations embodied in critical articles and reviews.

Unless otherwise indicated, Scripture quotations are from the ESV® Bible (The Holy Bible, English Standard Version®), copyright © 2001 by Crossway, a publishing ministry of Good News Publishers. Used by permission. All rights reserved.

Library of Congress Control Number: 2025931438

ISBN: 978-1-959145-28-8 (paperback)
         978-1-959145-29-5 (ePub)
         978-1-959145-30-1 (Kindle)

25   26   27   28   29   30   6   5   4   3   2   1

Ordinary Means, Extraordinary Ends

*Word, Sacrament,
and the Great Commission*

Edited by

Camden M. Bucey

Contents

Abbreviations vi

Preface vii

1. To the Ends of the Earth: The Great Commission and God's Unfolding Plan for the Nations 9
   Camden M. Bucey

2. Missions and the Gospel of God: Romans 1:8–17 25
   James J. Cassidy

3. The Kingdom of Power and the Great Commission: Matthew 28:18 37
   Lane G. Tipton

4. Mission Imperative: Christ's Command to Make Disciples in Matthew 28:19a 61
   Camden M. Bucey

5. The Deep Well and Lively Works of Christian Baptism:
   Matthew 28:19b 75
   R. Carlton Wynne

6. The Church's Mission Is Teaching: Matthew 28:20a 101
   James J. Cassidy

7. Jesus, the God Who Is with Us
   to the End of the Age: Matthew 28:20b 119
   Douglas B. Clawson

Appendix: Reformed Forum and Global Theological
   Education 137

Scripture Index 147

Abbreviations

ESV	English Standard Version
KJV	King James Version
WCF	Westminster Confession of Faith
WLC	Westminster Larger Catechism
WSC	Westminster Shorter Catechism

Preface

THE GREAT COMMISSION stands as both a mandate and a promise. Christ commands his church to make disciples of all nations, yet he does not leave us to this monumental task alone. He promises his presence and power until the end of the age.

This volume arose from two significant gatherings in 2024 where pastors and theologians explored the depths and implications of Christ's commission to his church. Two of the chapters originated as addresses at a pre-conference event prior to the Greenville Presbyterian Theological Seminary conference in Taylors, South Carolina, on March 5, 2024. The remaining chapters are adapted from addresses delivered at the Reformed Forum Theology Conference held at Hope Orthodox Presbyterian Church in Grayslake, Illinois, on September 28, 2024.

As these chapters demonstrate, the Great Commission is not merely a historical artifact from the early church—it is a living commission that propels the church forward today.

While the task may seem daunting, Christ has equipped his church with everything needed for this global mission. We need not resort to novel methods or pragmatic strategies. The Lord has provided spiritual means perfectly suited for this work: the ministry of Word and sacrament, empowered by his Spirit.

The appendix outlines Reformed Forum's mission and vision, particularly as it relates to global theological education. This material helps situate our organizational efforts within the broader context of Christ's commission to his church.

My prayer is that readers will be stirred to action by engaging with these chapters. May we be encouraged that Christ's commission endures, challenged to participate in this great work, and comforted that he is with us always as we advance his kingdom.

Camden M. Bucey
December 2024

1

To the Ends of the Earth

*The Great Commission and
God's Unfolding Plan for the Nations*

Camden M. Bucey

Presbyterians trace their theological and ecclesiastical roots back to Scotland. The nineteenth century in Scotland was a golden age of missions, wherein emboldened believers sought to bring the truths of the Reformation to the world according to the Great Commission.

One important chapter of Presbyterian missions occurred in the parish of Kilsyth, where a powerful vision for the nations was born. Here, William C. Burns, a child of Scotland, would inherit a legacy of faith that propelled him far beyond the confines of his homeland, to the distant lands of Manchuria—contemporary northeast China and inner Mongolia.[1] His final resting place, marked as "the advanced post of Christian conquests,"[2] serves as a testament to the enduring spirit of the Great Commission that has compelled generations of believers. This spirit, deeply rooted in "the Puritan hope" so heartily captured by Iain Murray in his classic book of that title,[3] was not confined to the shores of Britain but extended its reach to the ends of the earth through the faithful labor of Scottish missionaries. Alexander Duff, speaking with fervor in 1854, echoed this sentiment, challenging the church to grasp the promises of God with a faith that could move mountains, believing that even the most formidable bastions of idolatry could be brought low before the gospel.[4] William Carey delivered a similar clarion call to the church, urging believers to "expect great things from God; attempt great things for God."[5]

---

1. "Wm. H. Burns ministered for fifty-nine years, commencing in 1800, and in his long pastorate at Kilsyth he saw a great spiritual harvest such as James Robe had witnessed in the same place in the 1740s. It was his son, William C. Burns, who died in far-off Nieu-chwang in 1868, one of the most outstanding of all the first missionaries to China's millions. The work done in parishes like Ferintosh and Kilsyth moulded the men who were to be the leaders of Scottish missionary endeavour." Iain Hamish Murray, *The Puritan Hope: A Study in Revival and the Interpretation of Prophecy* (Edinburgh; Carlisle, PA: Banner of Truth Trust, 1975), 164.

2. Murray, 157.

3. Murray, *The Puritan Hope*.

4. Alexander Duff, *Speech of the Rev. Dr. Duff, on Foreign Missions and America, Delivered in the General Assembly of the Free Church of Scotland, on the Evening of May 29, 1854* (Edinburgh: J. Greig, & Son, 1854), 19; Murray, *The Puritan Hope*, 158.

5. Iain Murray quoting William Carey, who was summarizing Isaiah 54:2–3. Murray, *The Puritan Hope*, 140.

The Great Commission

Throughout this book, we intend to focus not merely upon the general subject of missions, but upon the Great Commission—our Lord's mandate to the church, which directs our mission unto his glorious return. As we engage this topic, let us remember the legacy of these missionaries, who dared to envision a world transformed by the power of the gospel. Their stories remind us that we are part of a continuum of faith, called to engage in the same mission, standing on the same promises of our Lord.

> And Jesus came and said to them, "All authority in heaven and on earth has been given to me. Go therefore and make disciples of all nations, baptizing them in the name of the Father and of the Son and of the Holy Spirit, teaching them to observe all that I have commanded you. And behold, I am with you always, to the end of the age." (Matt. 28:18–20)

This is a word given to the church upon the resurrection of our Lord, yet it is a command in service of the fulfillment of God's covenantal purpose which he established in the beginning. With that in mind, what does it mean to "go and make disciples of all nations"? To answer this question with the depth it deserves, we must place it within the sweeping storyline of the Bible—from the garden of Eden to the new Jerusalem. This is not merely a New Testament injunction but the climactic mandate of a covenant history that stretches back to creation itself.

In the Scriptures, we see a God who is neither distant nor disinterested but one who actively pursues his people, confirming his promises through covenants. From God's original offer to Adam in the covenant of works and then his promise of the seed of the woman after Adam fell in sin, to the covenant with Abraham, promising that through his seed all nations of the earth would be blessed, to the new covenant in Christ's blood, God has been unfolding his plan to redeem a people for himself from every tribe, tongue, and nation. This grand narrative of God's covenantal dealings forms the backbone of our exploration. And it is in this narrative that the Great Commission finds its rightful place as the capstone of God's redemptive plan.

A Vision of the Guaranteed Future and the End of Missions

The prophet Isaiah gives us a vision of the future when God's purposes for the nations will finally be realized.

> It shall come to pass in the latter days that the mountain of the house of the LORD shall be established as the highest of the mountains, and shall be lifted up above the hills; and all the nations shall flow to it, and many peoples shall come, and say: "Come, let us go up to the mountain of the LORD, to the house of the God of Jacob, that he may teach us his ways and that we may walk in his paths." For out of Zion shall go forth the law, and the word of the LORD from Jerusalem. He shall judge between the nations, and shall decide disputes for many peoples; and they shall beat their swords into plowshares, and their spears into pruning hooks; nation shall not lift up sword against nation, neither shall they learn war anymore. (Isa. 2:2–4)[6]

God's holy presence often rested on mountains—whether

---

6. See also Micah 4:1–4.

Mount Ararat (Gen. 8:4), Moriah (Genesis 22), Sinai (Exodus 19–Numbers 10), and even Eden (Ezek. 28:13–15). But of all these mountains, Mount Zion was the place where God put his name (1 Kings 11:36; 14:21; 2 Kings 21:4).[7] And the Spirit's work is not complete until Mount Zion is the exclusive location of worship.

In his vision, Isaiah sees the Lord reigning from Mount Zion in the new heavens and new earth (see also Isa. 65:17–25). On that day, the house of the Lord will be established as the highest of the mountains. It will be the place of preeminence over the whole earth. The Lord will conquer his enemies, and Mount Zion will be the clear location of the true king. All other mountains will be made low (Isa. 40:4), and worship from all peoples will be at the mountain of the Lord rather than the mountains of pagan gods.[8] All of God's people will have been reconciled into one new man (Eph. 2:11–15), because all of God's people—whether Jew or Gentile—will have been grafted into Christ.[9]

This is a vision of the guaranteed future and the end of missions. It is the end in the sense that all the elect will be called into God's house and they will all know him. We will have no further need to evangelize. Yet, it is also the end in that this is the purpose and goal for which we engage in missions. It is the reason for missions in the first place. Now that we know the ending, let us consider in greater detail how this plan and

---

7. See T. Desmond Alexander, *New Dictionary of Biblical Theology* (Downers Grove, IL: InterVarsity Press, 2000), 589.

8. See especially Mic. 4:1–2; cf. Isa. 2:2–3; 4:1–5; 25:6–26:2; Ezekiel 40–48; Rev. 21:9–10; G. K. Beale and D. A. Carson, *Commentary on the New Testament Use of the Old Testament* (Grand Rapids, MI: Baker Academic, 2007), 1151.

9. See Eph. 1:22; 2:20; 5:23; 1 Pet. 2:6; Isa. 28:16; Col. 1:18.

purpose unfolds throughout redemptive history and the beginning of the nations in the Old Testament.

Old Testament Anticipation

The Descendants of Noah and the Tower of Babel

In the aftermath of the flood, Genesis 9:18–19 introduces us to a seminal moment in redemptive history: "The sons of Noah who went forth from the ark were Shem, Ham, and Japheth.... From these the people of the whole earth were dispersed." This brief passage marks the inception of the nations, setting the stage for understanding how God's redemptive plan would unfold through diverse peoples and cultures. The lineage of Japheth is of particular interest for our study.

Japheth's descendants, listed in Genesis 10:2–5, are traditionally understood to have spread into the regions that would become Europe and parts of Asia. This expansion is not merely an historical or geographical note but carries profound theological significance. The dispersion of Japheth's descendants symbolizes the early formation of Gentile nations, which would later become pivotal in the narrative of Scripture as it unfolds to reveal the inclusion of the Gentiles in God's salvific plan. The blessing pronounced by Noah on Japheth in Genesis 9:27, "May God enlarge Japheth, and let him dwell in the tents of Shem," hints at a future integration and blessing of the Gentile peoples with the lineage of Shem—the line through which Abraham and, ultimately, Christ would come. This intermingling of blessings forecasts the gospel's reach beyond the boundaries of Israel to the entire world.

This providential widening of blessings, however, encounters a pivotal moment in the Tower of Babel narrative found in

Genesis 11:1–9. Humanity, speaking a single language, sought to make a name for themselves by building a city and a tower reaching to the heavens. This act of hubris, aiming to unify humanity apart from God, led to a divine intervention by which God confounded their language, resulting in the scattering of peoples across the earth. Babel stands as an example of human sinfulness—our tendency to seek autonomy from God and unity on our terms, which ultimately leads to division and dispersal.

The Abrahamic Covenant

Immediately after this account of rebellion in Genesis 11 comes the genealogy of Shem, which leads to the figure of Abram.

> Now the LORD said to Abram, "Go from your country and your kindred and your father's house to the land that I will show you. And I will make of you a great nation, and I will bless you and make your name great, so that you will be a blessing. I will bless those who bless you, and him who dishonors you I will curse, and in you all the families of the earth shall be blessed." (12:1–3)

This covenant is not a mere footnote in biblical history but a foundation upon which much of God's subsequent dealings with his people are built. It sets the trajectory for God's redemptive plan, which culminates in the person and work of Jesus Christ and continues through the church's obedience to the Great Commission. When God calls Abraham out of Ur of the Chaldeans, he is essentially inaugurating the next chapter in redemptive history, one that will carry significant implications for the nations—or, as the promise puts it, "all the families of the earth."

Israel as a Light to the Nations

While the promise focuses on the descendants of Abraham, the people of Israel, Scripture makes it increasingly clear that God's covenant promises were never intended solely for a particular ethnic or geographical community. From the very beginning, these promises had a universal scope, aimed at bringing blessing to all the families of the earth. We see this developed in multiple ways throughout Isaiah's prophecy.

Take, for instance, Isaiah 42:6–7, in which the servant of the Lord is commissioned not merely to be a blessing to Israel but to act as a "light for the nations." This servant is given the divine task to "open the eyes that are blind, to bring out the prisoners from the dungeon, from the prison those who sit in darkness." This theme is amplified in Isaiah 49:6, where God declares that it is "too light a thing" for the servant only to restore Israel. Instead, his mission is to be a light to the nations so that God's "salvation may reach to the end of the earth." This global vision anticipates the Great Commission, in which God commands us to make disciples of all nations, echoing the divine intent to bring salvation to the far reaches of the globe.

Later, in Isaiah 60:1–3, Israel is called to "Arise, shine, for your light has come," a light so compelling that it draws "nations" and "kings" to its brightness. Though Israel often faltered in its charge, the promise remained, finding its ultimate fulfillment in Jesus Christ—the true Israel and the light of the world. The church is now commissioned to reflect this light, drawing people from every tribe, tongue, and nation to the brilliance of the gospel.

As the prophetic voice of Isaiah casts a vision of the Abrahamic promises reaching their fulfillment, we find ourselves on the precipice of a critical juncture. The mission, grounded firmly in the covenant promises of God, anticipates a glorious future where the knowledge of the Lord permeates the world as the waters cover the sea (Isa. 11:9). This eschatological vision, brimming with hope, prepares us for the pivotal moment in the history of salvation—the incarnation of the promised Messiah.

New Testament Fulfillment

The Coming of the Messiah

The transition from the Old to the New Testament is more than a turn of the page; it is the dawning of a new era in God's redemptive narrative. In this epoch, the "fullness of time" heralded by the prophets is realized (Gal. 4:4). God's sovereign timing unfolds with the birth of his Son, a singular event that is both rooted in history and eternal in significance.

This coming is the fulfillment of a lineage of promises, a succession of prophecies, and a series of types, all converging in Christ. His advent is not a detached episode, but the axis upon which the whole of redemptive history tilts, affirming every divine utterance as "Yes" and "Amen" in him (2 Cor. 1:20). As we witness this fulfillment, we find ourselves not only as heirs to the promises but as witnesses to the faithfulness of God, whose redemptive work reaches its zenith in the person and work of Jesus Christ.

Jesus inaugurated a new covenant that would be the means by which God's blessings would reach the ends of the earth. In his life, death, and resurrection, Jesus fulfilled the law and the prophets, becoming the true Israel, the true servant, the true light to the nations. In him, the promises to Abraham and the visions of Isaiah reach their ultimate fulfillment. Through faith in Jesus, all nations of the earth are blessed as people from every tribe and tongue become children of Abraham by faith (Gal. 3:16–29).

This is not an artificial imposition upon the text of the Old Testament. Jesus identified himself with Isaiah's prophecies. When he walked into the synagogue, picked up a scroll, and read from Isaiah 61, he declared Isaiah's prophecy to have been fulfilled that day (Luke 4:16–30). He is the one who will deliver the people from their bondage. In Jesus Christ, then, we see the system of Old Testament promises not merely converging but coming to life. He is the living embodiment of these promises, the one in whom the storylines of covenant history find their resolution. Through him, the particularities of Israel's history are opened up to include people from every nation, fulfilling God's promise to bless all families of the earth.

This is the vision of the end that Isaiah provides. In Isaiah 2:3, many peoples will say, "Come, let us go up to the mountain of the LORD, that he may teach us his ways and that we may walk in his paths." Those who walk in the way of the Lord arrive at Mount Zion, coming to worship the king. So great is the Lord's call, that these nations are depicted as streams flowing up the mountain.

And they come to the Lord to be taught. The purpose of the teaching is that they will walk in his paths—that they would learn from him and obey his commandments. This is deeply aligned with the mission of the church as articulated in the Great Commission—to make disciples of all nations, baptizing them in the name of the Father, the Son, and the

Holy Spirit, and teaching them to observe all that Christ has commanded. In this mission, the church serves her risen and ascended King, empowered by his Spirit, to bring the light of the gospel to a world enshrouded in darkness.

Christ's earthly ministry, therefore, is not an endpoint but a glorious beginning. It marks the inauguration of the church's mission, fueled by the Spirit working through the Word, to bring Christ's kingdom to the ends of the earth. This new age of Spirit-enabled mission breaks forth at Pentecost.

The Apostolic Mission

The day of Pentecost in Acts 2 marks the gathering of the nations through the outpouring of the Holy Spirit. Jerusalem was filled with devout Jews "from every nation under heaven." When the Holy Spirit descended on the people, they each began to speak in other tongues and were enabled to hear the gospel each in their own language. This miraculous event signifies the reversal of Babel's curse. Pentecost demonstrates that the unity God desires is not found in human achievement or uniformity but in the Spirit-filled proclamation of Jesus Christ, reconciling us to him and to each other in righteousness and holiness.

From Babel's scattering to Pentecost's gathering, Scripture reveals God's masterful plan to redeem a fractured humanity, uniting us not through human effort but through the transformative power of the gospel. With the ascension of Christ and the descent of the Holy Spirit at Pentecost, the apostles were thrust into a new phase of God's covenantal plan. Empowered by the Spirit, these ordinary men were tasked with an extraordinary mission: to be Christ's witnesses "in Jerusalem, and in all Judea and Samaria, and to the ends of the earth" (Acts 1:8).

Pentecost is a foretaste of the new heavens and the new earth, where people from every tribe, tongue, and nation will worship the Lamb (Rev. 7:9).

The Apostolic Mission in Acts and the Pauline Epistles

As the apostles and other early believers spread out from Jerusalem, we see them wrestling with how to apply the Old Testament Scriptures and Jesus's teachings in new contexts. The council of Jerusalem in Acts 15 serves as a pivotal moment in this regard. The apostles and elders gathered to discuss the issue of Gentile inclusion, ultimately affirming that Gentiles are not bound by the Mosaic law in order to be part of God's covenant community. This decision reflects a nuanced understanding of redemptive history, recognizing that the gospel is not bound by ethnic or cultural barriers.

Paul, the apostle to the Gentiles, is particularly concerned with the proper articulation and application of the gospel in diverse settings. Whether he was addressing the legalism of the Galatians or the licentiousness of the Corinthians, Paul consistently grounded his arguments in the redemptive work of Christ and the overarching story of God's covenantal promises. One of Paul's recurring themes is the "mystery" that has now been revealed—namely, that Gentiles are fellow heirs in the same body of Christ (Eph. 3:6).

Paul was called to bring the gospel to the Gentile world, effectively serving as the primary instrument through which the descendants of Japheth were invited to dwell in the spiritual tents of Shem. In Romans 9–11, Paul articulates God's purpose in electing Israel and his sovereign plan to include the Gentiles in his redemptive purposes. This is seen specifically in Romans 11:11–24, where he employs the metaphor of an olive tree, illustrating how Gentiles have been grafted into the covenantal blessings initially given to Israel. This inclusion is not a replacement but an enlargement, reflecting the prophecy concerning Japheth and the expansive grace of God that reaches beyond ethnic and national boundaries.

This reminds us that God's plan for salvation was always designed to encompass all nations, pointing to the fulfillment of this plan in Christ Jesus. The church today is commissioned to continue extending the reach of the gospel to the ends of the earth, inviting all peoples to find their place in God's house, under the lordship of Christ. Just as Japheth's descendants were foreknown to dwell in the tents of Shem, so now, through Christ, all are invited to dwell in the presence of God, participating in the blessings of the covenant and our eternal inheritance.

This is the vision of the future we saw in Isaiah 2. What a glorious day that will be! While we do wait for this future day, we enjoy this already in anticipation. Hebrews 12 declares that, "you have come to Mount Zion and to the city of the living God, the heavenly Jerusalem . . . and to God, the judge of all, and to the spirits of the righteous made perfect, and to Jesus, the mediator of a new covenant. . ." (vv. 22–24).

Conclusion

From the promise to Abraham that in him all families of the earth would be blessed, to Isaiah's vision of the nations streaming to Christ on the heavenly Mount Zion, we see a God who is steadfast in his commitment to redeem a people for himself from every tribe, tongue, and nation. As it did for the ancient church, this continuity in God's redemptive plan ought to inform and inspire our own Reformed and Presbyterian congregations even as it did our forefathers in Scotland. The seeds sown by William C. Burns and his fellow missionaries continue to bear fruit from Kilsyth to China. Their lives, marked by an unwavering commitment to the gospel, remind us that the call to missions is not a relic of the past but a living, breathing mandate for the church today. On this note, Alexander Duff's impassioned plea to the General Assembly of the Free Church of Scotland rings as true today as it did in 1854.

> Oh, what promises are ours, if we had only faith to grasp them! What a promise is that in the great commission — Go and do so, and lo I am with you, even to the end of the world! We go forth amongst the hundreds of millions of the nations, we find gigantic systems of idolatry and superstition consolidated for 3,000 years, heaped up and multiplied for ages upon ages, until they tower as high mountains, mightier than the Himalaya.... But what does faith say? Believe and it shall be. And if any Church on earth can realize that faith, to that Church will the honour belong of evangelizing the nations, and bringing down the mountains.[10]

The legacy of these Scottish missionaries challenges us to look beyond our immediate context and consider our role in God's global mission. Let us carry forward the torch of faith, inspired by those who have gone before us. In this grand narrative, we are not mere spectators but active participants, striving with all his energy until the earth is filled with the knowledge of the glory of the Lord, as the waters cover the sea (Isa. 11:9). May we, too, be emboldened by the Spirit, and continue

---

10. Duff, *Speech of the Rev. Dr. Duff, on Foreign Missions and America, Delivered in the General Assembly of the Free Church of Scotland, on the Evening of May 29, 1854*, 19; Murray, *The Puritan Hope*, 158.

the work of the Great Commission in our generation.

2

Missions and the Gospel of God

Romans 1:8–17

James J. Cassidy

The work of the church is missions, period. Everything the church is called to do is summarized in the biblical injunction to preach the Word (2 Tim. 4:2). While preaching is not the church's only activity, everything the church does either points to the gospel preached or serves the ministry of the gospel preached. Everything the church does is either missions itself, a sign and seal of missions, or serves its mission.

The basic life of the church is summarized in Acts 2:42:

"And they devoted themselves to the apostles' teaching and the fellowship, to the breaking of bread and the prayers." This represents Word, sacrament, and prayer. Later, mercy ministry would be added to the church's activity, but that too serves the mission of the church. Consider Acts 6:2–4, 7: "It is not right that we should give up preaching the word of God to serve tables. Therefore, brothers, pick out from among you seven men of good repute, full of the Spirit and of wisdom, whom we will appoint to this duty. But we will devote ourselves to prayer and to the ministry of the word. . . . And the word of God continued to increase, and the number of the disciples multiplied greatly in Jerusalem." While mercy ministry is a vital responsibility of the church and is inherently good, it serves the church's primary mission. Through mercy ministry, the Word of God increases and disciples multiply.

Turning to Romans 1, the apostle Paul had already introduced the gospel of God in verses 1–7. He explained both its nature and its subject. It concerns Jesus Christ, the Son of God, who was descended from David according to human flesh. Paul identified himself as an apostle called by Christ, specifically commissioned to preach the gospel to the Gentiles. Paul's missionary heart and ministry were fully displayed as he opened his heart to the Roman believers. In doing so, he revealed his love for the Gentile world. His love was so profound that he endured great suffering to reach them with the gospel.

This brings us to our text in Romans 1:8–17. We can examine it in four parts: missions and Paul's prayers (vv. 8–10), missions and Paul's edification of the saints (vv. 11–12), missions and Paul's evangelization of the Gentiles (vv. 13–15), and missions and justification by faith alone (vv. 16–17).

Missions and Paul's Prayers

First, Paul begins his letter with thanksgiving to God. "First" (Rom. 1:8)—or "to begin with"—he thanks God. This pattern of beginning with encouragement to the church is characteristic of Paul. Leading with doxology and glorifying God, he expresses gratitude for them. Significantly, he offers his thanks "through Jesus Christ" (Rom. 1:8). This *through* indicates mediatorship. Paul approaches God, even in thanksgiving, through Jesus, the only mediator between God and man. Sinners cannot approach God in prayer through their own righteousness, having none. Our sin would only offend God and provoke his wrath. We need a sinless mediator to bring our prayers before the Father. For Paul, that mediator is Jesus Christ alone.

Paul's thanksgiving stems from their faith being proclaimed throughout the world—that is, their faith being well known among all churches scattered throughout the Gentile nations. What makes their faith particularly noteworthy? The church in Rome was, by all accounts, the farthest church from Jerusalem at that time. Though Paul was the apostle to the Gentiles, he had not even visited Rome yet! Nevertheless, a church was already established there. The gospel's spread to such distances was remarkable—the reaching of the empire's capital with the gospel was indeed significant.

Paul is so passionate about the Roman saints that he calls God as his witness to his truthfulness. For he serves God—with his spirit—in the gospel of his Son. Serving God with his spirit indicates serving with all his heart—a sincere, wholehearted service without reservation (Rom. 1:9). Moreover, it is service in the gospel. This is Paul's primary ministry—gospel service.

Yet his work extends beyond preaching. He serves the gospel through unceasing prayer for them. This does not indicate that he literally prays without interruption, but rather that he maintains regular, persistent prayer for them. His specific prayer request is that somehow—by God's will—he might come to them (Rom. 1:10). The journey to Rome was no small undertaking—not merely a Mediterranean cruise! Additionally, Paul was heavily engaged in ministering to his planted churches. Nevertheless, he yearns to participate in the mission to the Gentiles in Rome. His eagerness for ministry among them drives his prayer for successful passage there. God would eventually answer this prayer, though perhaps not as Paul envisioned—delivering him to Rome not on a luxury cruise liner but on a prison ship!

The key lesson here is the vital connection between prayer and missions. The church must pray for mission opportunities and for ways to reach the nations. When we pray—through Jesus Christ—we should expect God to make a way. Then we go forth to preach the gospel and make disciples, fulfilling the Great Commission. Prayer exists to serve missions.

Missions and Paul's Edification of the Saints

Second, Paul expresses a deep longing to see the Christians in Rome. His desire is to "impart some spiritual gift" (Rom. 1:11). This gift is spiritual because it characterizes the age—the age of the Holy Spirit, who is given to the church by the ascended Christ. The Holy Spirit bestows heavenly gifts upon his people—gifts that originate in heaven and are not carnal in nature. These are not corruptible gifts, but incorruptible. Such gifts can strengthen the believers in Rome. This strengthening is not physical, but spiritual—accomplished by the power of the Holy Spirit.

We might ask how Paul intends to strengthen them. Though we will examine this in more detail later, he provides the answer in Romans 1:15—Paul is eager to preach the gospel to them. He will strengthen them through gospel preaching. This reveals a crucial truth: preaching the gospel strengthens believers. It never becomes outdated or irrelevant. The Christian never graduates beyond the gospel.

When Paul seeks to edify the church, to strengthen it, he envisions the Word accomplishing this work. The strengthening comes from the Holy Spirit, who works with and through the Word to fortify believers. Importantly, it is the gospel as preached that strengthens believers. While believers are indeed strengthened in other ways—through fellowship, prayer meetings, Bible reading, and the sacraments—all these elements either flow from or serve the gospel. As the Westminster Confession of Faith states, the primary means God provides "for the gathering and perfecting of the saints" is the preaching of the holy gospel (25.3).

Yet the benefit Paul desires to bring is not one-directional. He anticipates mutual edification. As he imparts a spiritual gift to them, his own faith is strengthened. This is a familiar experience: when you meet a fellow believer or converse with another church member during fellowship about the things of the Lord, both parties are mutually encouraged. You walk away refreshed and renewed.

The key lesson here is that strengthening existing believers is as crucial to the church's mission as evangelizing unbelievers. Making disciples is a process: while converting unbelievers is the first step, strengthening believers is the ongoing work of disciple-making.

Missions and Paul's Evangelization of the Gentiles

Third, Paul shares what we might call inside information. This information concerns his intentions to visit them. For the Roman church, the prospect of a visit from the apostle Paul would have been momentous. He explains that he has been prevented thus far, occupied with planting churches and bringing relief to those suffering famine in Jerusalem (Rom. 1:13).

Paul's desire is clear—he wants to reap a harvest. This picturesque metaphor of harvest appears throughout the New Testament to signify the ingathering of lost souls. Part of the harvest he envisions is among the existing believers in the church. He wants to reap a harvest "among you" (v. 13)—the harvest that results from imparting spiritual gifts, manifesting in strengthened faith among believers.

But there is another harvest in view. He also seeks to reap among "the rest of the Gentiles" (v. 13). While this could refer to unsaved Gentiles in Rome, Paul likely has a broader vision. "The rest of the Gentiles" may well encompass all Gentile lands. Not that Paul expected to preach to every non-Jew or visit every Gentile territory, but he recognized there were more souls to gather and churches to plant throughout the Gentile world. This broader interpretation aligns with Paul's statement at the end of Romans, where he reveals his intention to use Rome as a launching point for preaching the gospel as far west as Spain (Rom. 15:24, 28). His goal is to extend the gospel's reach as widely as possible among the Gentiles.

In Romans 1:14, Paul explains the source of this missionary drive: he is obligated to both Greeks and barbarians, wise and foolish. This obligation comes directly from the Lord (Acts 9:15). Paul is compelled by Christ's call to minister to all manner of unbelievers without discrimination. The Greeks represent the sophisticated philosophers, while the barbarians represent the uncouth and foolish. These categories—and everyone between—are the objects of Paul's ministry. Yet Paul's motivation extends beyond mere obligation, as Romans 1:15 reveals: He is eager to preach the gospel in Rome. He is no hireling or mercenary, laboring under compulsion alone. While indeed compelled by his calling from Christ and desires to please his master, he does so willingly and joyfully. The lesson here is clear: the church must genuinely desire to bring the gospel to all peoples. She must be prepared and eager to reach even the most unlikely or challenging unbelievers.

Missions and Justification by Faith Alone

Fourth, Paul declares he is not ashamed of the gospel (Rom. 1:16), knowing it possesses power. Or more precisely, the gospel *is* the power of God. The gospel is good news of what God himself has accomplished for sinners' salvation. The salvation in view here is specifically God's saving work in Christ.

It is crucial to note that this salvation is "to everyone who believes" (v. 16). We must interpret Paul correctly here. He is not presenting faith as another kind of work, nor suggesting that God accepts faith in place of works. Rather, the gospel proclaims that salvation is already accomplished—completed once for all. It cannot be completed, activated, or earned by our faith. The gospel announces what has already happened. Nevertheless, God-gifted faith unites us to the Christ who accomplished our salvation, and through that union, all the benefits of his work are applied to us.

This universal scope is clear in Paul's statement "to the Jew first and also to the Greek" (v. 16). This salvation extends to all kinds of sinners, not restricted to Jews but embracing Gentiles as well. The phrase "to the Jews first" does not indicate special effectiveness for Jews, but rather historical priority. The gospel was promised to them from ancient times, beginning with Abraham. Yet even before Abraham, the gospel was promised to Adam. It was then given to Abraham not solely for his descendants, but through his seed, for "all the families of the earth" (Gen. 12:3). Historically, the gospel was preached first in Israel, then in Samaria, and finally to the nations. It is to the Jew first, but also to the Greek—offered freely and indiscriminately to all (Rom. 1:16).

This connection between missions and justification by faith alone is crucial. While justification has always been by faith alone since Genesis 3, this truth particularly matters for understanding the church's mission. The Pharisaical party within the churches would have required Gentile believers to follow the law for full acceptance by God. Such a requirement would have completely halted the church's disciple-making mission. The law demanded not just circumcision but also citizenship in Israel's theocracy and numerous ceremonial practices, including the requirement to attend Passover in Jerusalem—a task practically impossible for most Gentiles in Rome or beyond. Instead, what missions requires is simple: the gospel preached, water, wine and bread, and—in obedience to the Lord's command—the prayers of the saints. That can be done anywhere—and everywhere!

As Paul later explains in Romans 10, the righteousness of the law requires complete obedience, including proper pilgrimages and sacrifices in Jerusalem. But the word of faith needs no such long journeys! It is near to all, even in distant lands. For anyone—Greek, barbarian, Roman, or even American—

who confesses Christ as Lord and believes in their heart will be saved (v. 9). Justification comes not to those who perform the law of Moses, but to those whose hearts God sovereignly changes through his monergistic grace. This faith—not works of the law—is the instrument of justification for both Jew and Gentile.

In Romans 1:17, Paul explains why he is not ashamed of the gospel: it reveals "the righteousness of God." This phrase "the righteousness of God" is crucial—it is the theme of Romans. But what does it mean? Two interpretations have been proposed: either God's righteous character or the righteousness God gives for sinners' justification. The context clearly supports the latter, as Paul's immediate concern is how both Jews and Gentiles are justified apart from the Law.

The gospel thus reveals the mystery hidden for ages (Rom. 16:25)—how God can be just while justifying sinners (Rom. 3:26). Consider this: a just God must, by nature, condemn sinners. Yet sinners live on, and many will be forgiven. How can God forgive sins without compromising his righteousness? A just judge must punish sin; God does not arbitrarily forgive. Two steps are required for God to be both just and justifier.

First, sin must be punished in someone other than the sinner. Christ bears our punishment on the cross. Since he was sinless, our sin had to be imputed to him—he was reckoned a sinner and judged for our sins. Second, we must receive a righteousness not our own. Our sins are removed, but we still need positive righteousness—the perfect, sinless record of Jesus imputed to us. This is the righteousness revealed in the gospel. Paul says it is revealed "from faith for faith" (Rom. 1:17)—a phrase variously translated but best understood as emphatic: the gospel is revealed for faith *alone*. It belongs to a person not by works of the Law but by faith alone. Habakkuk 2:4 confirms this: "The righteous shall live by faith"—or the one who is righteous by faith will live. True Israel—Jews and Gentiles—receives eternal life by grace, through faith in Jesus Christ.

The lesson is clear: Justification by faith alone perfectly suits the church's spiritual mission. The church, no longer bound to one nation, is a spiritual institution ministering to people from all nations, who are fully included in God's covenant not by law-keeping but by justifying faith alone.

Concluding Thoughts

From all this, I would like to offer three concluding thoughts. First, the church needs to understand her mission. Second, the church must not deviate from her mission. Finally, the church must trust the Lord in her mission.

First, the church needs to understand her mission. The church is called to go forth and make disciples of all nations. This mission is spiritual in nature. The gift it seeks to impart is Spiritual (Rom: 1:11), which I have capitalized because it is of and from the Holy Spirit. This gift was bestowed upon the church at Pentecost. This is an irrevocable gift to the church and an eschatological one. It is the kind of gift God gives to the church in these last days, for the church now resides in the age of the Spirit, and her gifts correspond to this age.

The mission of the church differs fundamentally from that of the church under Moses. The Mosaic commission was not to make disciples of the Gentiles but to smite them. Israel was to show no mercy, taking up carnal weapons for warfare. But the church's mission is Spiritual. Having received the Spirit's gift, she imparts it to others—not through worldly weapons or ways, not through political power or clever schemes, but through the message the world considers foolish—the message of the cross.

The church fulfills her mission when she faithfully and indiscriminately preaches the gospel of God's Son. Her mission, like Paul's, is to reap a harvest among the Gentiles. This happens through Word and Spirit alone. The church's mission is not to convert states or transform cultures, but to gather and perfect the elect. Whether through many or few, God saves his own through the church's preaching ministry. This is the essence of our mission.

Second, the church must not deviate from her mission. The church must maintain Paul-like focus and zeal for preaching the gospel to all. We are not called to preach only to "the deserving"—those deemed worthy or those like us. The gospel must go to Greeks and barbarians, to the wise and foolish alike. Though the world around us lies in darkness, a wicked and perverse generation, we must love and pity our wicked neighbors. Like Paul, we are under obligation to them. Though they may oppose us and stand at enmity with God, we must never stand against them—even as we stand against sin. Like Paul, we must be for them, desiring their salvation rather than destruction.

We must pity, pray for, and preach to both barbarian and fool. What providence offers us today! While Paul traveled far to bring the gospel to the nations, we minister in a country where the nations come to us. Whatever your political views, consider the opportunity before the church. As the nations come, let us preach the gospel to them without wavering, staying steadfast on course!

Finally, the church must trust the Lord in her mission. We

face temptation to seek other means for bringing about the obedience of faith. But Paul remained focused, committed to imparting spiritual gifts, strengthening believers, and reaping a harvest through gospel preaching. We might be tempted to think that behavioral modification or education alone will produce obedience among Gentiles—as if we could transform the foolish into wise and refine barbarians into Greeks. We may be tempted to minimize preaching. People dislike being "preached at." They find sermons boring or irrelevant. So we might offer entertainment instead of sermons, or success tips instead of the gospel—anything to draw people in.

But observe Paul's trust in the Lord and in God's appointed means for the church's mission. He trusts that the preached gospel suffices to gather and perfect the saints. Here lies our mission. Our gospel confidence rests on God's promise to bring harvest from it and our trust in the God of the gospel himself. Amen.

3

THE KINGDOM OF POWER AND THE GREAT COMMISSION

Matthew 28:18

LANE G. TIPTON

THE TEXT OF Matthew 28:18–20 supplies what the church has universally termed the Great Commission from the Lord Jesus Christ:

And Jesus came and said to them, "All authority in heaven and on earth has been given to me. Go therefore and make disciples of all nations, baptizing them in the name of the

Father and of the Son and of the Holy Spirit, teaching them to observe all that I have commanded you. And behold, I am with you always, to the end of the age."

The specific mandate involves a Christ-commanded and Christ-enabled authority for ministers of the gospel to make disciples and baptize those from all nations who are called by the Spirit through the gospel and to teach them all that Christ has commanded. The ground for this great mandate rests in the fact that Jesus—the giver of the mandate—as raised from the dead and especially *as ascended to the right hand of God in heaven*, has been given all authority in heaven and on earth. Comprehensive in scope and totalizing in demand, this mandate defines the central task of the church in this age: to serve as the instrumental means by which Christ himself throughout this age, by his Spirit working through his Word, gathers and perfects his elect scattered throughout the earth.

The commands in verses 19–20 are bracketed by two grand promises—one in Matthew 28:18 and the other at the very end of verse 20: "All authority in heaven and on earth has been given to me" and "Behold, I am with you always, to the end of the age." These twin truths supply the church with the infallible confidence that the Great Commission will succeed in its mission to gather and perfect the elect from the four corners of the earth.

Five summarizing propositions capture the central point expounded in this chapter. First, the eternal Son possesses his kingly office by an eternal appointment from the Father in the counsel of peace (also known as the *pactum salutis*). Second, Jesus as the incarnate Mediator was given "all authority in heaven and on earth" at the precise moment he was exalted to the right hand of the Father and received what traditional Reformed theology terms the "kingdom of power." Third, the kingdom of power serves the entirely unique spiritual relation he enters into with his church by his Word and Spirit, what traditional Reformed theology has termed the "spiritual kingdom," or the "kingdom of heaven." Fourth, Jesus's kingly work in the Great Commission consists most basically in a gathering of his people on earth as he conforms them through his Spirit and by his Word to his glory in heaven in a two-age movement, what we will term following Meredith Kline, a "heavenizing" movement. Fifth, this two-age movement of heavenizing the church through the Great Commission repeats the pattern of Christ's own two-estate translation from earth in the estate of humiliation to heaven in the estate of glory.

These propositions, when understood in their proper order and proportion, prove incompatible with any view that proposes a weakened understanding of Jesus's present dominion only for that dominion presumably to increase during a so-called future millennial kingdom (premillennialism) or golden age (postmillennialism). This chapter contends that Jesus Christ already exercises unlimited dominion that will continue throughout this age until he destroys all dominion and authority and power at the end of this age when he inaugurates the kingdom of glory.

Official Kingship and the "Counsel of Peace"

Geerhardus Vos, in his discussion in the *Reformed Dogmatics* regarding the kingly office of Jesus Christ, begins by making a critical distinction between the "essential rule" of the eternal Son of God and his "personal rule" given his official kingly appointment as Mediator. Vos discloses the nature of the kingly office of the Mediator in question and answer 93: "What is the kingly office of the Mediator? His official appointment and activity on behalf of God to rule and protect His church."[1] Jesus Christ has received an official appointment from the Father to a kingly office as the Mediator. That official appointment focuses directly on his ruling over and protecting the church. Yet that raises a further obvious question: Does not the Son of God, given his eternal deity, already possess such royal dominion as king over all creation? And if so, is he not king apart from his official appointment as the Mediator? Vos continues,

> 94. Is Christ already king apart from His mediatorship? The answer: Yes. As sharing in the Divine Being, He also possesses from eternity the royal power over all creation that belongs to God. This continues with His true deity through all that befalls Him. In a strict sense, however, one cannot speak of this as a *munus regium*, a "kingly office." After all, an office always presupposes delegated authority exercised in the name of another. Divine kingly power is absolute. Hence one was accustomed to speak of a *regnum essentiale*, an "essential rule," and place next to it the *regnum personale*, the "personal rule." The latter, then, means the official kingship of the Mediator.[2]

Vos observes in that passage an important and traditional Reformed distinction. On the one hand, given his deity, the eternal Son of God has an essential rule over all created things. The essential rule accrues due to fact that he is God-of-himself (essentially) and Son-from-the-Father (personally). On the

---

1. Geerhardus Vos, *Reformed Dogmatics*, ed. Richard B. Gaffin Jr., trans. Richard B. Gaffin Jr., vol. 3 (Bellingham, WA: Lexham Press, 2012–2016), 175.
2. Vos, *RD*, 3:175.

other hand, the "official kingship of the Mediator" is a "delegated authority exercised in the name of another." As Son from the Father in the eternal processions, he receives an appointment from the Father in the eternal missions. Vos accordingly distinguishes between an authority eternally tethered to the deity of the Son (an essential rule) and an authority eternally delegated to the Son (an official rule).

Vos further explains that the "delegated authority" that comprises the "official kingship of the Mediator" arises in the "counsel of peace." Vos says, "Christ received this kingship when He was appointed as Mediator in the counsel of peace. As far as its essence is concerned, it was not tied to the actual performance of His suretyship, for this essence has existed from the first beginnings of the church on up to the incarnation as well as afterward."[3]

The counsel of peace, as developed in seventeenth-century Reformed orthodoxy, refers to an eternal arrangement among the persons of the Trinity. Francis Turretin, a seventeenth-century Reformed scholastic, played a significant role in developing and systematizing the eternal counsel of peace (*pactum salutis*). Turretin took the phrase "counsel of peace," from Zechariah 6:13, and argued that it refers to the eternal intra-Trinitarian agreement among the persons of the Trinity (there is an entire volume that could be written on the history of Reformed interpretation of that verse). God the Father, God the Son, and God the Holy Spirit, as living and immutable Trinitarian persons who are one God, eternally ordain salvation for the elect by the Father, in the Son, and through the Holy Spirit. In this eternal Trinitarian arrange-

---

3. Vos, *RD*, 3:175.

ment, the Father appointed the Son to be the mediator of God's elect, and promised him the fullness of the Holy Spirit, session at the Father's right hand in heavenly glory, and the glorious salvation of God's elect as the outcome of his official activity as Mediator.

The eternal Son of God—God of himself regarding his essence and Son from the Father regarding his person—voluntarily agreed to accept the official appointment as Mediator. While the doctrine of the counsel of peace does not divide the operations of the Father, the Son, and the Holy Spirit as one God, it does make explicit distinct terminal acts appropriate to each person—the Father ordains, the Son accomplishes, and the Spirit applies redemption. The unique terminal act that pertains to the Son is his appointment to a kingly office as Mediator. All the works of God outside of himself are one, but not all of the persons of the Godhead are Mediator.

To put the procession of the Son and the mission of the Son in its Trinitarian focus, the Son receives his personal existence from the Father in the eternal procession of generation, and the Son receives an official appointment from the Father as Mediator in the eternal counsel of peace (*pactum salutis*). His person proceeds from the Father in the eternal processions; his office proceeds from the Father's appointment in the eternal *pactum*. The order of the processions finds expression in the order of the *pactum*. In his eternal procession, we grasp his essential rule over all things as God-from-himself and Son-from-the-Father. In the eternal *pactum*, we discern an official appointment from the Father to rule over all things for the church as Mediator.

In the counsel of peace, the eternal Son of God is freely given and freely receives his appointment as Mediator to discharge all of the responsibilities that attend such an official appointment. So, the official appointment of kingship over the church begins in the *pactum*, but it is not executed until immediately after the fall. The essence of his office exists eternally, but the execution of that office occurs in time. The official rule of the Son of God as Mediator finds its *eternal* expression in the counsel of peace (*pactum salutis*) and finds its first *historical* expression immediately after the fall of Adam and Eve into sin. Therefore, Christ's official rule as King over the church finds its first historical expression immediately after the fall of Adam and Eve into sin and endures throughout every administration of the covenant of grace (Gen. 3:15ff.).

How does this initially relate to the Great Commission? Given that he is God-from-himself and the Son-from-the-Father in the divine processions, he has all the *essential* resources needed to execute the Great Commission flawlessly. Given his official appointment as Mediator in the counsel of peace, he has all the *official* resources to fulfill the Great Commission. The foundation of the royal dominion of the Son of God, and the guarantee of the completion of the Great Commission, rest in the fullness of essential and official resources that are his as the appointed king over all things for the church.

Official Kingship and the *Regnum Spirituale*

Having discovered the eternal beginning of the Son's official kingship over all things for the church, what do we say about the execution of the responsibilities of that kingship in time and the specific relation the Son as King sustains to those over whom he is appointed king—namely, the church?

Regarding the nature of the relation established between

the appointed King and his redeemed vassals, Vos says, "It is called the *regnum spirituale*, the 'spiritual kingdom,' because it is established by spiritual means and is governed by spiritual power alone."[4] The means by which the Mediator exercises his royal dominion over the church comes by his Word and Spirit. He reveals his will in the Scriptures of the Old and New Testaments. He enables compliance with his revealed will by the irresistible grace of his Spirit. Vos continues, "All office-bearers in the church derive their authority from Him and receive their appointment from Him. Nothing can be done with authority without this authority being granted by Him."[5] Officers in the church are the instrumental means by which Christ exercises his authority from heaven. He empowers their work and puts their ordinary means to the extraordinary end of advancing his spiritual kingdom. Vos says that Christ's redeemed vassals, "enter into a wholly unique relationship with Him. They are no longer their own possession but with body and soul the possession of Jesus Christ. Faced with His will, they have none but only unqualified submission. Whether they live or die, they are the Lord's. In this way, the believer stands in a totally unique relationship to Christ."[6]

Let me make some comments about this spiritual relation, this spiritual kingdom, and its King—the Mediator Jesus Christ. First, the relation of the King to his vassals is unique. Its uniqueness rests in the spiritual character of the relation—a relation initiated and sustained by the Spirit of God and regulated by the Word of God. From the divine side, the relation is sealed by the work of the Holy Spirit, and from the

---

4. Vos, *RD*, 3:175.
5. Vos, *RD*, 3:175.
6. Vos, *RD*, 3:176.

human side, the Spirit works "unqualified submission" to the King. Christ rules his church in a unique spiritual relation by his Spirit working through his Word.

Second, the spiritual relation forges a spiritual kingdom. Vos observes, "It is a spiritual kingdom, but that notwithstanding, a real kingdom. That is, no external physical force is used, as is the case with the kingdoms of this earth.... There is authority, power, and sovereignty—in the first instance in Christ and then entrusted by Him to His servants."[7] The spiritual kingdom is a real kingdom of authority and power. It is the holy realm where Christ rules as King by the power of his Spirit and by the authority of his Word. The spiritual kingdom consists in all who are joined to Christ by the Spirit and through faith. Vos says that the spiritual kingdom "belong[s to] all those whom He has redeemed or if according to the rule of the word of God we have to assume that to be the case; therefore, all believers."[8] Thus, the spiritual kingdom belongs to those called out of the nations (not nations as geopolitical units) who offer the King unqualified submission and worship.

Third, the spiritual kingdom, and the reign of its King, endures forever. The spiritual kingdom reaches back to the very first believers—Adam and Eve—and it will remain the same into eternity. Vos says, "As soon as there were believers, the exercise of dominion by the Mediator began.... Also, for the future, this kingdom will remain the same for all eternity as to its essence. It cannot cease to exist any more than believers can cease to be the property of their Savior. As Christ is Priest and Prophet forever, so also will He be King eternally (Psa 89:4,

---

7. Vos, *RD*, 3:176.
8. Vos, *RD*, 3:177.

36–37; Luke 1:33; Dan 2:44–45)."[9]

The spiritual kingdom consists in an entirely unique relation initiated and sustained by the Spirit of Christ, regulated by the Word of Christ, and includes all of those who are called out of darkness into the light of Christ. Within this spiritual kingdom, traditional Reformed theology has drawn a further distinction between the kingdom of grace (*regnum gratiae*) and the kingdom of glory (*regnum gloriae*). The kingdom of grace begins on the day of the fall of Adam and Eve and the beginning of the covenant of grace. It consists of believers and their children. It can also include unbelievers who enter by baptism mixed with a false profession of faith. The kingdom of glory begins at Jesus's second coming. The latter begins on the day of judgment. It will include all and only believers. Vos says that in the kingdom of glory, "Christ will no longer rule by providing Himself with servants but will exercise His kingly power in His own person. His power will be perfected in His subjects, and nothing more will be lacking in the full unfolding of the kingdom of heaven."[10]

Without at this point addressing the interface between the kingdom of grace and the kingdom of glory in this age, we need to appreciate that both involve an unfolding of the "kingdom of heaven." Vos offers us a wonderful summary of the kingdom of heaven: "It is well known that the designation 'kingdom of heaven,' usually occurs in Matthew's Gospel. In Mark and Luke, one only finds 'kingdom of God.' . . . The addition 'of heaven' serves to indicate the *heavenly origin* and the *heavenly character* of this dominion. The Mediator, who was

---

9. Vos, *RD*, 3:178.
10. Vos, *RD*, 3:178–179.

anointed as King, was *in heaven from eternity and has returned to heaven, and heaven is the center of all His activities.*"[11]

The kingdom of heaven unfolds in every epochal movement of the kingdom of grace, and the "full unfolding" of the kingdom of heaven will occur at Christ's glorious and visible second coming. The spiritual kingdom that moves from a kingdom of grace to a kingdom of glory is itself the unfolding in redemptive history of the kingdom of heaven. The eternal Son was anointed king in the eternal counsel of peace. The eternal Son was enthroned as king in heaven in the absolute beginning of Genesis 1:1. The incarnate Son returned to heaven to sit there at the Father's right hand. Thus, heaven is the center of all his present activities.

In summary terms, the official kingship of the eternal Son of God as Mediator begins in the eternal counsel of peace, expresses itself in his enthronement in heaven in the absolute beginning, and unfolds in redemptive history as a kingdom of grace (this age) and a kingdom of glory (age to come). He departed from heaven in humiliation only to return to heaven in exaltation—all his activities in history are the unfolding of the kingdom of heaven—even as heaven is the "center of his activities."

Official Kingship, the *Regnum Potentiae*, and Unlimited Dominion

As we turn to the Great Commission itself, Vos makes one last distinction of great interest to us regarding the official kingship of Christ: As ascended and seated at the right hand of the Father in heaven, he has received the *regnum potentiae* or "the

---

11. Vos, *RD*, 3:180, emphasis added.

kingdom of power." Vos says, "The *regnum potentiae*, the kingdom of power . . . extends over the entire universe. According to Matthew 28:18, to Him has been given all authority in heaven and on earth."[12] The incarnate Mediator has by virtue of his exaltation received from the Father absolute authority in heaven and on earth. He has received the "kingdom of power" that consists in an absolute, comprehensive, totalizing authority in the upper (heavenly) and lower (earthly) registers.

Precisely when did Jesus enter into the kingdom of power? Vos incisively summarizes,

> The apostle says that God has seated Christ at His right hand in heaven, far above all rule and authority and power and dominion and every name that is named, not only in this but also in the coming world (Eph. 1:20; cf. further Phil. 2:9–10; and Psa. 8, with Heb. 2:6–9). Concerning this kingdom of power, we should note: That Christ has not always possessed it but first received it after His ascension, when He went to sit at the right hand of God. The spiritual kingdom has always existed from the first beginning of the church; this kingdom of power began with the third stage of Christ's exaltation.[13]

That last sentence supplies the critical point. The spiritual kingdom has always existed in the sense that the Son was appointed as King over the church in the counsel of peace and has exercised his spiritual kingship from the first beginning of the church after the fall. But the "kingdom of power began with the third stage of Christ's exaltation." The first stage of Jesus's exaltation emerged in his bodily resurrection from the

---

12. Vos, *RD*, 3:181.
13. Vos, *RD*, *3:181.*

dead on the third day. The second stage of Jesus's exaltation occurred forty days later in his bodily ascension into heaven. The third stage of Jesus's exaltation occurred when he entered bodily into heaven to sit as encoronate at the right hand of God in heaven.

From his seat at the right hand of God, "all of his activities are centered in heaven." He speaks from heaven as prophet. He serves in heaven as high priest. He rules from heaven as king. All of his activities as Mediator therefore find their epicenter in heaven. Therefore, the "third stage" of Jesus's exaltation—his session at the right hand of the Father in heaven—not only makes heaven the center of all his activities but also inaugurates the kingdom of power. Several biblical texts speak of this kingdom of power:

> I saw in the night visions, and behold, with the clouds of heaven there came one like a son of man, and he came to the Ancient of Days and was presented before him. (Dan. 7:13)

> Jesus said to him, ". . . But I tell you, from now on you will see the Son of Man seated at the right hand of Power and coming on the clouds of heaven." (Matt. 26:64)

> And Jesus said, "I am, and you will see the Son of Man seated at the right hand of Power, and coming with the clouds of heaven." (Mark 14:62)

> . . . and what is the immeasurable greatness of his power toward us who believe, according to the working of his great might that he worked in Christ when he raised him from the dead and *seated him at his right hand in the heavenly places, far above all rule and authority and power and dominion, and*

above every name that is named, not only in this age but also in the one to come. And he put all things under his feet and gave him as head over all things to the church, which is his body, the fullness of him who fills all in all. (Eph. 1:22–23; emphasis added)

In light of the survey of these texts, we are in position to grasp the significance of Acts 2:32–33, "This Jesus God raised up, and of that we all are witnesses. Being therefore exalted at the right hand of God, and having received from the Father the promise of the Holy Spirit, he has poured out this that you yourselves are seeing and hearing." The outpouring of the Spirit begins the climactic stage in the unfolding of the kingdom of heaven and comprises the first expression of the kingdom of power all in the service of the Great Commission. Jesus Christ, as seated at the right hand of the Father, pours out the Spirit from heaven and breathes out his Word through the apostles in his initial acts that begin the fulfillment of the Great Commission.

This text also sheds great light on the two texts that bracket the Great Commission: "All authority in heaven and on earth has been given to me" (Matt. 28:18) and "I am with you always, to the end of the age" (Matt. 28:20). The official entrance into the kingdom of power dawned in Christ's exaltation at the right hand of the Father (Acts 2:33). The official expression of the kingdom of power manifested as Christ poured out the Holy Spirit whom he received from the Father—what both Peter and Paul term "the Spirit of Christ" (Rom. 8:9b; 1 Pet. 1:11)—the Spirit belonging to and poured out by Jesus Christ on the day of Pentecost.

Acts 2:32–33 seamlessly integrates the kingdom of power

and the spiritual kingdom. Having been exalted to the right hand of the Father (kingdom of power), he pours out the promised Holy Spirit (the spiritual kingdom). This is the beginning of Christ's work in the Great Commission. The "kingdom of power" ensures that nothing in heaven or on earth can stop the successful completion of the Great Commission as the "spiritual kingdom" of heaven advances by the Spirit of Christ working through his Word—his gospel. The kingdom of power therefore serves the spiritual kingdom—the spiritual rule of Christ over his church by his Word and Spirit.

Vos says further that in the kingdom of power Jesus Christ receives as ascended and encoronate in heaven consists in an "unlimited dominion" that serves to advance the spiritual kingdom in the Great Commission. He says, "The specific purpose of this all-encompassing kingship is found in the spiritual kingship that Christ has over His Church; Ephesians 1:22, 'and gave Him as Head over all things to the church.' This entails: (1) Christ is the Head of the Church; (2) as such He is above all things, exercises unlimited dominion."[14]

The purpose of the all-encompassing kingship of Jesus Christ emerges in the "spiritual kingship" of Christ over his church (the kingdom of grace)—the people with whom he enters into a totally unique spiritual relation and the place where he dwells with a totally unique spiritual presence. The exercise of unlimited dominion therefore serves concretely and specifically the welfare of his body, the church.

Jesus Christ, in terms of his "third stage" of exaltation—seated at the right hand of the Father in heaven—*presently* exercises unlimited dominion as he establishes and expands

---

14. Vos, *RD*, 3:181.

his spiritual kingdom. There is no future earthly millennial reign where he will come (in the future) to exercise unlimited dominion. There is no future golden age where he will come (in the future) to exercise unlimited dominion. The unlimited dominion of the Lord Jesus Christ operates now as he has received the kingdom of power and the name above every name and the power above every power in this age and in the age to come. The possession of unlimited dominion for Jesus Christ is not reserved for some future earthly millennial reign or some "golden age" on earth prior to Jesus's second coming. The unlimited dominion of Jesus Christ consists in a present, ongoing, uninterrupted, and absolute power that he exercises from heaven as the exalted King. It is not the case that he will have more dominion in a future golden age, as suggested both by the title and the argument in Kenneth Gentry's *He Shall Have Dominion: A Postmillennial Eschatology*.[15] That view fundamentally depreciates or obscures the unlimited dominion Christ presently possesses as ascended and encoronate at the Father's right hand in heaven. Views that weaken the present dominion of Christ in this age in order to magnify his future dominion in this age obscure if not deny that Jesus now, as exalted and enthroned, possesses unlimited dominion in his official identity as king over the church.

So, if there is no future millennial kingdom or golden age where Christ comes in this age to have some greater dominion than he presently possesses, to what end does he now have unlimited dominion? That is the amillennial question.

---

15. The first edition of *He Shall Have Dominion* was published by The Institute for Christian Economics (Tyler, TX: January 1, 1992). A third expanded and revised edition was published by Victorious Hope Publishing (San Francisco, CA: February 22, 2021).

Vos continues,

> More specifically, this unlimited dominion is necessary to protect the Church from its enemies. The Church is in the midst of the world and still has the evil of the world in its own bosom. So, if it is to be secure, then its Head must have dominion over the world. Its history is intertwined with the history of the world. Consequently, only (he) who governs the latter will be able fully to lead the former. Christ has therefore assumed dominion over the world for the benefit of His Church. He exercises it on behalf of God, for this kingdom of power, too, is and remains an official kingdom. That Christ received this kingdom of power at the same time had consequences for His spiritual kingdom, since, as the exalted God-man, He can now by His Spirit also work everywhere in order to assert even the power of His exalted humanity.[16]

Jesus Christ now exercises his kingdom of power for the sake of and in the service of the spiritual kingdom—the kingdom of grace and glory. All authority in heaven and on earth has been given to me (kingdom of power) so that all of the elect from all the nations might be discipled—gathered and perfected—in the church (the spiritual kingdom). The *regnum potentiae* serves the *regnum spirituale*.

One last point regarding the *regnum potentiae* or "kingdom of power" needs to be appreciated. Vos summarizes, "That it will cease when its goal is reached. This is taught by the apostle in 1 Corinthians 15:24, 28. In the end, the Son will hand over the kingdom to the Father when He will have destroyed all dominion and authority and power, in order then also to be

---

16. Vos, *RD*, 3:181.

subjected Himself to the One who has subjected all things to Him, so that God may be all in all."[17] The unlimited dominion of Christ in his mediatorial "kingdom of power" exists from when he assumed his seat at the Father's right hand in heaven until the consummation of the spiritual kingdom at the end of the age. The "kingdom of power" exists in undiluted fullness until the revelation of Christ's climactic act of destroying "all dominion and authority and power" at the end of this age. So, it is not the case that unlimited dominion is presently withheld from Jesus only to be attained in the future millennial kingdom or golden age. Rather, the unlimited dominion Jesus presently possesses will be given a final expression on the last day—the consummation of his spiritual kingdom. This means, then, that Christ's destruction of "all dominion and authority and power" at the *end* of this age proves to be the climactic expression of his present "unlimited dominion" *throughout* this age.

The Great Commission and the Two-Age Movement of Heavenization

How do the "kingdom of power" and the "spiritual kingdom" relate to the kingdom of heaven—where heaven is the "center of all Christ's activities?" His kingly work from heaven consists in a *two-age work of translating the church into heaven—the center of all his activities in this age and in the age to come*. Christ, working by his Spirit and through his Word, is gathering to himself in this age all of the elect from the four corners of the earth and is conforming them to his image as the glorified king of heaven. We can call Christ's gathering and perfecting

---

17. Vos, *RD*, 3:181.

of his people—this discipling of the elect from every nation through the teaching and baptizing ministry of the church—*a heavenizing movement*—a translational movement that transforms and conforms the church to the earthly cross and the heavenly glory of King Jesus.

Jesus Christ, as ascended and encoronate, is the man of heaven (1 Cor. 15:47). Jesus Christ, as ascended and encoronate at the Father's right hand, has entered heaven as the forerunner of his church (Heb. 6:20). Appropriately, the church is now raised with Christ and seated with him in heavenly places (Eph. 2:6), has "come to Mount Zion" in heaven (Heb. 12:22), where its life is "hidden with Christ in God" (Col. 3:3). Christ's work in the Great Commission consists in a gathering and perfecting of his people as he translates them to the center of all his activities—heaven itself. However, sharing in the heavenly glory of Jesus in this age is tethered to suffering in Christ (Rom. 8:17), "always carrying in the body the death of Jesus, so that the life of Jesus may also be manifested in our bodies" (2 Cor. 4:10), sharing in his sufferings and "becoming like him in his death" (Phil. 3:10), taking up the cross, denying self, and following Jesus daily (Luke 9:23).

Yet Christ, by the same Word and Spirit, will in the age to come receive his church into heaven on the glorious day of bodily resurrection. WLC 90 says that on the last day, believers will "be received into heaven, where they shall be fully and forever freed from all sin and misery; filled with inconceivable joys, made perfectly holy and happy both in body and soul, in the company of innumerable saints and holy angels," and the church will see with resurrected eyes and hearts the glory of God in the face of Jesus Christ and find "the perfect and full communion . . . Christ in glory." Paul speaks of it as being caught up in the air to meet the Lord in the clouds (1 Thess. 4:17). Vos notes the idiom of meeting the Lord "in the clouds" entails a "remoteness from the surface of the earth."[18] Being caught up in the air to meet the Lord in the clouds involves ascending into heaven itself (see Rev. 21:2 for the imagery of the heavenly Jerusalem descending to meet the ascending church).

Meredith Kline argues that in the final act of consummation the very good earth and the redeemed of God will be "heavenized" as the heavenly Jerusalem descends to envelop, transform, and conform the earthly to the heavenly.[19] He observed that "those who are glorified are thereby equipped for the perception of and participation in the Glory-dimensioned realm. Newly opened to them, heaven is for them a new place, whatever objective alterations of the cosmos do or do not follow upon the final judgment.... This gathering of redeemed, glorified mankind into heaven changes heaven; it introduces the pleroma of Christ's body, the church, into the heavenly scene."[20] In this glorious final movement of heavenizing consummation, God in Christ will free the church from all sin and misery and confer glory without suffering, joy without sorrow, and communion with God liberated from sin and death.

This two-age heavenizing act of conforming the church to her heavenly King bears the same pattern as manifested in the earthly and heavenly estates of the Mediator—an historical movement from earthly suffering to heavenly glory. The

---

18. Geerhardus Vos, *The Pauline Eschatology*, (Phillipsburg, New Jersey: P&R, 1994), 136.
19. Meredith G. Kline, *God, Heaven and Har Magedon: A Covenantal Tale of Cosmos and Telos* (Eugene, OR: Wipf & Stock Publishers, 2006), 27–28.
20. Kline, *God, Heaven and Har Magedon*, 215–216.

two-estate movement from earthly suffering to heavenly glory in the work of the incarnate Mediator finds replication in a two-age movement from earthly suffering to heavenly glory for the church in union with the incarnate Mediator (see Rom. 1:3–4; 8:17–24).

Religious Hope and the Two Grand Indicatives

Jesus brackets the Great Commission with two grand indicatives—two grand statements of fact that are true of Christ in his spiritual relation to his church. These twin truths supply the deepest religious hope for the church in this present age as she undertakes the Great Commission—either directly in the special office of minister or indirectly in other special and general offices.

The first emerges in Matthew 28:18, "All authority in heaven and on earth has been granted to me." As raised, ascended, and especially as enthroned in heaven, Jesus Christ has unlimited dominion over all things in heaven and on earth. There are so many unhelpful presentations of Jesus as our incarnate Lord circulated in evangelical theology today. Jesus Christ, as the incarnate and glorified Mediator, possesses an absolute authority over the invisible heavens and visible earth. He has no limitations in power, no limitations in dominion, and no limitations in authority. In Vos's language, Jesus Christ presently possesses an "unlimited dominion" as the God-man, seated at the right hand of God in heaven.

The second emerges in Matthew 28:20, "And behold, I am with you always, to the end of the age." This refers to the spiritual union between Christ and his church—the indwelling of his Spirit—and his personal presence with his church at every moment of her suffering during this present evil age. By his Spirit, Christ dwells in the hearts of those in his spiritual kingdom, the church. Ephesians 3:16–17 says, "that according to the riches of his glory he may grant you to be strengthened with power through his Spirit in your inner being, so that Christ may dwell in your hearts through faith." For the Spirit to dwell in the inner self is for Christ to dwell in our hearts. Being in Christ, sharing in Christ, is also a fellowship with the Holy Spirit mediated by the Holy Spirit. There is no sharing in Christ that is not also a fellowship with the Holy Spirit. Romans 8:9–10 teaches the same glorious truth: if the Spirit dwells in you (v. 9), then Christ is in you (v. 10). For the Spirit to be in you is for Christ to be in you and *vice versa*. Union with Christ is a Spirit-wrought union, such that Christ is in you and you are in Christ, even as the Spirit is in you and you are in the Spirit.

The relation between these twin truths means that the incarnate person of the Mediator, who has unlimited dominion, also dwells in the heart of the Christian in a most intimate spiritual union by faith. The unlimited dominion *of* Christ and the intimate spiritual union *with* Christ are inseparably joined in the Great Commission. Unlimited dominion over all things in heaven and on earth as seated in heaven; personal indwelling in you and with you to the end of the age by the Spirit—both are true of your exalted King.

In Jesus Christ, then, exalted to the right hand of the Father and given the Spirit without measure, you find the glorious and mysterious fulfillment of Isaiah 57:15, "For thus says the One who is high and lifted up, who inhabits eternity, whose name is Holy: 'I dwell in the high and holy place, and also with him who is of a contrite and lowly spirit, to revive the spirit of the lowly, and to revive the heart of the contrite.'" In union with this Christ—the King with unlimited dominion who dwells in you and with you by his Spirit to the end of this age—go forth and serve him and "be steadfast, immovable, always abounding in the work of the Lord, knowing that in the Lord your labor is not in vain" (1 Cor. 15:58).

4

MISSION IMPERATIVE

*Christ's Command to Make Disciples
in Matthew 28:19a*

CAMDEN M. BUCEY

HAVING ALREADY CONTEMPLATED the authority that Christ has received, our attention now turns to the words of our Lord in Matthew 28:19a: "Go therefore and make disciples of all nations." Jesus, having all authority in heaven and on earth (Matt. 28:18), directs his disciples—and through them, the entire church—to engage in a mission that spans the globe. It is a command that compels us here and now to step out in faith, leaving behind the comfort of familiar surroundings to enter the world with the life-giving message of the gospel. Verse 19a provides the dynamic forward thrust of the gospel, urging us to carry the message of Christ to all nations, peoples, and languages. Through the church's Spirit-wrought obedience, these people will hear the gospel and be brought into the covenant.

The global nature of the Great Commission reflects the scope of God's redemptive plan, which extends to every corner of the earth. As Isaiah prophesied, "all the ends of the earth shall see the salvation of our God" (Isa. 52:10). This challenges us to lift our eyes beyond our immediate context and see the vast fields that are ripe for harvest (John 4:35). It propels us outward, into a world that desperately needs the light of the gospel, and it reminds us that we cannot just take or leave our Lord's words here in Matthew 28. It is the central mission of the church, given by the risen Christ who holds all authority and promises his continual presence as we advance.

A Missional Necessity: "Go"

Christ's Authority and the Call to Go

When we examine the original Greek of the Great Commission in Matthew 28:19–20, we discover an important detail that is not immediately apparent in our English translations. There is only one imperative in the text: "make disciples" (μαθητεύσατε; *mathēteusate*). This verb is in the aorist active imperative, which is a command for the church to carry out. It is directed to the church collectively (hence, second person plural), highlighting the shared responsibility of the church in fulfilling this mission.

The word μαθητεύσατε carries the full weight of the Great Commission. Everything else in the passage is a presupposition, prerequisite, or qualifies what it means to "make disciples." The actions of going, baptizing, and teaching are the means through which disciples are made. We have confidence in this mission because Christ has all authority in heaven and on earth, and he is always with us. But the primary command—the heart of the Great Commission—is to make disciples. This means that the church's mission is not merely about evangelism or conversion but about forming followers of Christ who are committed to learning from him and growing in obedience to his commands.

In the original language, the word "go" (πορευθέντες; *poreuthentes*) is not an imperative verb but a participle. This grammatical structure sheds light on the relationship between "going" and the imperative to "make disciples." While the participle in Greek does not carry the force of a command in the same way as an imperative verb, the grammatical structure shows that the action of going is a necessary part of making disciples. In other words, one of the ways the church fulfills the imperative to make disciples is by going into the world.

The passive voice of πορευθέντες further emphasizes that this going is not self-initiated. It reflects a sense of being sent, of being carried forward by another's authority and power—namely, Christ's. We are not going on our own initiative, but we are being propelled by Christ's authority and his commission. Moreover, the participle is in the nominative plural form, meaning that it applies to a collective group—the disciples, and by extension, the church. The task of going and making disciples is not for individual Christians alone, but for the whole church.

Thus, while "make disciples" is the central command, "going" is how this command begins to be carried out. It's a "mission necessity." The church is sent into the world to make disciples, and this going takes place under the authority and power of Christ, who directs and sustains his church in this mission. This interconnectedness of going and disciple-making reminds us that the Great Commission is not fulfilled in one place alone. It requires the church to be active, to move outward, and to bring the gospel to the ends of the earth.

The Global Scope of the Command

The call to "go" in the Great Commission is deeply rooted in the broader biblical narrative, particularly in the covenantal promises of God that unfold throughout Scripture. In Genesis 12:2–3, God calls Abram (later Abraham) and makes a series of promises to him: "I will make of you a great nation, and I will bless you and make your name great, so that you will be a blessing. I will bless those who bless you, and him who dishonors you I will curse, and in you all the families of the earth shall be blessed." This covenant establishes Abraham as the father of a nation that will be uniquely set apart to serve God. But even from the beginning, the focus of the covenant is not limited to Abraham's descendants alone. The promise is that "all the families of the earth" will be blessed through Abraham and his offspring. This promise finds its ultimate fulfillment in Jesus Christ, the seed of Abraham (Gal. 3:16). Through Christ's death and resurrection, the blessing of salvation is extended to the nations, fulfilling God's promise that all peoples of the earth would be blessed through Abraham's line.

The Great Commission, then, is the means by which this blessing is made known and applied to the nations. The church is called to go into the world and proclaim the gospel, bringing the blessing of salvation to those who are far off and near. The Great Commission is, in many ways, the continuation of

God's covenantal promise to Abraham. The call to "go" is the church's participation in God's unfolding plan of redemption, which began with the promise to Abraham and reaches its climax in Christ. The church, as the spiritual descendants of Abraham, is tasked with bringing the message of Christ—the fulfillment of that covenant promise—to all nations.

Moreover, the Great Commission reflects the global scope of God's redemptive plan. The promise to bless all nations through Abraham points to the inclusion of the Gentiles in God's covenant people. In the Old Testament, this promise is seen in glimpses, as Gentiles are drawn to the God of Israel. But in the New Testament, with the coming of Christ, this promise is fully realized as the gospel goes out to the nations, breaking down the dividing wall of hostility and bringing Jews and Gentiles together in one body (Eph. 2:14–16).

Thus, the call to "go" in the Great Commission is not just about geographic expansion; it is about the fulfillment of God's covenantal promises to bless all nations through Abraham's seed. It is about the church participating in the grand narrative of redemption, taking the message of Christ to the ends of the earth, so that people from every tribe, tongue, and nation may come to know the blessing of salvation in Christ. We see this in Revelation 7:9, where John sees "a great multitude that no one could number, from every nation, from all tribes and peoples and languages, standing before the throne and before the Lamb." This is the ultimate goal of the Great Commission—that people from every corner of the globe would worship Christ together in the new heavens and new earth.

The Missional Imperative: Make Disciples
The Imperative of Discipleship (Matthew 28:19a)

It is a mission necessity that the church to go into the world. It's the "mission imperative" to make disciples. Everything else in the Great Commission—going, baptizing, and teaching—serves this central task of making disciples. The Greek word μαθητεύσατε carries a rich meaning that extends beyond evangelism and conversion. To make disciples involves more than bringing people to faith in Christ; it means nurturing them in that faith, helping them grow as followers of Jesus who are committed to learning from him and obeying his commands. It is not enough simply to spread the gospel message and move on; making disciples requires an ongoing investment in the lives of believers, guiding them toward spiritual maturity. The task of disciple-making is a holistic endeavor that encompasses both the initial act of bringing people to Christ and the lifelong process of helping them grow in their relationship with him.

To accomplish this task of making disciples, Jesus gives us three participles that describe the means by which this mission is fulfilled: going, baptizing, and teaching.

1. Going (πορευθέντες; *poreuthentes*): As we have already discussed, "going" is the first step in making disciples. The gospel must be taken to the nations, and the church must be willing to move outward, crossing cultural, geographical, and linguistic barriers to bring the good news of Christ to all people. This act of going is the initiation of the disciple-making process, as the church brings the gospel to those who have not yet heard it.

2. Baptizing (βαπτίζοντες; *baptizontes*): Baptism is the sac-

ramental sign of our incorporation into Christ and entrance into the covenant community. It marks the beginning of a disciple's pilgrimage, signifying their union with Christ and their inclusion in the body of believers. Dr. Wynne will cover this in his chapter.

3. Teaching (διδάσκοντες; *didaskontes*): Discipleship does not end with conversion or baptism. Jesus commands us to teach new disciples. The content of this teaching is comprehensive—it encompasses "all that I have commanded you," which we can understand as "the whole counsel of God" (Acts 20:27). Teaching is a lifelong endeavor that equips disciples to live in obedience to Christ and grow in spiritual maturity. Dr. Cassidy will cover this in his chapter.

Together, these three actions—going, baptizing, and teaching—form the framework for making disciples. Now, accomplishing this mission requires a sustained commitment to the entire process of disciple-making, from evangelism and conversion to baptism and lifelong teaching. This is the mission of the church: to make disciples of all nations, helping people come to know Christ, grow in their relationship with him, and live as his followers in every area of life.

Evangelism is, of course, a vital part of this mission. The proclamation of the gospel is the starting point of discipleship. Without the gospel being shared, people cannot come to faith in Christ. However, the Great Commission pushes us further than evangelism alone. The goal is not simply to see people make a one-time decision for Christ but to guide them into a lifelong journey of following him as his disciples.

The church, therefore, must see its mission as a holistic endeavor that includes not only the initial work of bringing people to faith but also the long-term work of nurturing that faith.

This requires a sustained commitment to teaching, mentoring, and walking alongside believers as they grow in their discipleship. The Great Commission is fulfilled not just when people come to faith but when they are made into mature, obedient followers of Christ who are able to teach others and make disciples themselves. In short, the church's mission is not completed when someone professes faith in Christ. The mission continues as the church nurtures that new believer, teaching them to observe all that Christ has commanded and helping them grow into mature disciples who will, in turn, go out and make disciples of others. This is the ripple effect of discipleship, and it is through this multiplication of disciples that the kingdom of God expands and flourishes.

A Missional Motivation: Christ Enables and Energizes His People

This brings us to our "mission motivation." Rev. Clawson will explore this further in his chapter as he writes of Christ being with his people to the end of the age. At this point, I would like to focus on a related theme in Colossians 1:28–29 and how Christ enables and energizes the church to present every person "mature in Christ."

Christ's Empowerment of His Laborers

The mission before the church is not one that we carry out in our own strength. Rather, it is Christ who empowers his people to fulfill this divine calling. This truth is vividly portrayed in Colossians 1:28–29, where the apostle Paul explains that his labor in ministry is not merely the result of his own efforts but is energized by the power of Christ working within him.

Paul writes, "Him we proclaim, warning everyone and

teaching everyone with all wisdom, that we may present everyone mature in Christ. For this I toil, struggling with all his energy that he powerfully works within me" (Col. 1:28–29). Here, Paul lays out his philosophy of ministry—a ministry that is centered on proclaiming Christ and focused on presenting every person mature in him. This goal of spiritual maturity parallels the Great Commission's emphasis on making disciples, who are not only brought to faith but are nurtured and taught to grow in their knowledge and obedience to Christ.

Paul's language in this passage emphasizes the intensity of his labor. We do not want to invest too much in etymology, but the word the English Standard Version (ESV) translates as "struggling" (ἀγωνιζόμενος; *agōnizomenos*) conveys the idea of striving, even agonizing, in pursuit of a goal. It is a focused, enduring struggle, much like an athlete striving to reach the finish line. But what is most important here is that Paul does not rely on his own strength in this struggle. He labors with "all his energy that he powerfully works within me."

This dependence on Christ's strength is critical for understanding how the church is to fulfill the Great Commission. Just as Paul labored to present every person mature in Christ, relying on the energy of Christ that worked powerfully within him, so too the church is called to make disciples through the power of Christ. This is not a task we can accomplish on our own. The work of disciple-making, from evangelism to teaching to nurturing spiritual growth, requires divine power.

The good news of the gospel is that Christ does not leave us to struggle alone. He gives us his Spirit, empowering us to carry out the mission he has entrusted to us. As Augustine famously prayed, "Give what you command, and then command whatever you will."[1] What he calls us to do, he also enables us to accomplish. We are not alone. Christ is with us, working in us and through us, enabling us to fulfill the Great Commission with the energy and power that he supplies.

Christ's Established Goal for His Laborers

The work of disciple-making is ultimately about spiritual growth and maturity, which is cultivated through the ongoing use of the ordinary means of grace—Word, sacraments, and prayer. The term *mature* (τέλειον; *teleion*) used by Paul points to a process of spiritual growth that moves toward completion, reflecting the full stature of Christ. It is a dynamic journey of becoming more like him. This involves not only learning biblical truths but also applying them to every area of life, growing in holiness, love, and obedience. It encompasses both the initial stages of faith and the lifelong process of sanctification, as believers grow into the fullness of what it means to be followers of Christ.

In this sense, the Great Commission's call to "make disciples" finds its fulfillment in presenting believers mature in Christ. The church's mission is not complete when someone makes a profession of faith; it continues as the church walks alongside believers, guiding them through the ordinary means of grace toward greater spiritual maturity. This involves consistent preaching and teaching of God's Word, participation in the sacraments, and prayer—activities that sustain and grow the believer in their relationship with Christ.

Paul's ministry philosophy, as expressed in Colossians

---

1. Augustine, *The Confessions*, ed. John E. Rotelle, trans. Maria Boulding, The Works of Saint Augustine: A Translation for the 21st Century. Part I, Books (Hyde Park, N.Y.: New City Press, 1997), Book X, 40, 263.

1:28–29, serves as a model for the church's mission today. He labors tirelessly, not just to see people converted but to see them grow in their faith, striving to present every person mature in Christ. This labor reflects the church's ongoing role in nurturing believers to spiritual maturity. As the church engages in disciple-making, it must do so with the goal of seeing believers transformed into the image of Christ, through the means of grace that he has provided. Thus, disciple-making begins with evangelism but extends far beyond it, encompassing the entire Christian life as believers are nurtured, taught, and guided toward spiritual maturity in Christ.

The Missional Means: The Role of the Ordinary Means of Grace in the Great Commission

How will this happen? This brings us to the "mission means." This process of nurturing believers requires the consistent and faithful use of the ordinary means of grace—the administration of the Word, sacraments, and prayer—through which Christ nourishes his people and brings them to maturity. This requires patience, perseverance, and a deep investment in the spiritual growth of each individual. This is where the church's mission of making disciples is truly lived out not only in bringing people to faith but cultivating their faith, helping them to grow in their knowledge of God and their obedience to his Word. In this way, the vision of presenting every person mature in Christ is the guiding principle of the church's mission. Everything we do in ministry should be directed toward this goal: that believers would grow into the full stature of Christ and be presented mature before him on the day of his return.

Conclusion: The End of Missions

This work will one day reach its glorious fulfillment. As referenced earlier, John depicts that day in Revelation 7:9–10, "After this I looked, and behold, a great multitude that no one could number, from every nation, from all tribes and peoples and languages, standing before the throne and before the Lamb, clothed in white robes, with palm branches in their hands, and crying out with a loud voice, 'Salvation belongs to our God who sits on the throne, and to the Lamb!'" This vision shows us the end goal of the church's mission—a redeemed people from every nation, tribe, people, and language, gathered together to worship Christ in the glory of the New Jerusalem (Isa. 2:1–4; Mic. 4:1–5).

This is the fulfillment of God's redemptive plan, a plan that began with the promise to Abraham that all the families of the earth would be blessed through his offspring (Gen. 12:3). This plan reaches its climax in the gospel of Jesus Christ, who has reconciled people from every corner of the earth to God through his death and resurrection. And it is through the church's faithful obedience to the Great Commission that this plan is brought to its completion.

As we look forward to this glorious day, we are reminded that our labor in the Lord is not in vain (1 Cor. 15:58). Our faithful labors today—energized by Christ's Spirit—contribute to the glorious future when all nations will be gathered into the kingdom of God, and Christ will be worshiped by a redeemed people from every tribe, tongue, and nation.

Every believer is called to participate in the work of spreading the gospel and making disciples, confident in Christ's presence and empowering work. Some may be called to go, physically entering the mission field—crossing borders, learning new languages, and engaging with different cultures to proclaim Christ to those who have never heard the gospel. Others may be called to send, supporting those who are on the front lines of mission work. This could mean financially supporting missionaries, praying for their efforts, or providing logistical support and encouragement to those who have gone out for the sake of the gospel. Sending is just as vital to the Great Commission as going. The church cannot accomplish its mission without those who faithfully send and support the work of missions around the world.

Others may support through active involvement in the local church's disciple-making efforts. This could mean mentoring new believers, teaching Sunday school, leading a Bible study, or living out the gospel in your daily life. The work of disciple-making begins at home, in your local community, and it requires faithful believers who are committed to nurturing others in their faith.

Whatever your role may be, know that you are part of something much bigger than yourself. The Great Commission is a corporate calling for the entire church, and every believer has a role to play. Whether you are going, sending, or supporting, you can be confident that Christ is with you, working through you to accomplish his mission. As you embrace your role in this mission, trust in his empowering work, and know that your efforts are contributing to the glorious future when all his people will be gathered into the kingdom of God.

5

THE DEEP WELL AND LIVELY WORKS OF CHRISTIAN BAPTISM

Matthew 28:19b

R. Carlton Wynne

On a mountainside in Montreat, North Carolina, there is a fountain of fresh spring water. The fountain is pretty unimpressive, really. It is just a metal pipe extending from a retaining wall. The retaining wall is set within a recessed grotto adorned with a small but thick cobblestone frame.

Despite its humble appearance, that fountain has captivated

my imagination since I was a young boy for one key reason: it is always flowing. For decades, I have seen people drive up to the fountain to fill water bottles, wash their faces, and enjoy the fountain's endless supply. I've brought my children to the fountain, and we usually to top off a Nalgene bottle or two before driving home to Georgia.

Year after year, the water flows because it is the product of profound natural forces. Rain and snow fall down from the heavens and, as the water percolates through layers of rock and soil in the Blue Ridge Mountains, it filters down into an underground reservoir. The composition of subterranean rock enriches the water with minerals, making it clear and drinkable. And then changes in elevation create pressure that forces the water back to the surface, and eventually out through the little spigot to the delight of parched pilgrims.

Christian baptism, I think, is a lot like that mountain spring. The waters of baptism run deep, and the benefits of baptism ceaselessly flow. The waters run deep because baptism is a sacrament that attends the new covenant, which, itself, arises from the ancient history of God's covenant dealings with his people. And baptism gives rise to ceaseless, lively works, or uses and functions, in the church today. The Great Commission (Matt. 28:18–20) itself shows us that covenant baptism is integral to the church's mission. But baptism does more. Baptism illuminates family life. It is efficacious for the elect. It instructs us in the gospel. It initiates discipleship, informs apostasy, and invigorates fellowship among God's people—and this is just a sampling of the many things God does through baptism.

As this chapter considers the third phrase of Jesus's commission for the church—"baptizing them in the name of the Father and of the Son and of the Holy Spirit" (v. 19b)—I want to zero in on the two sides of baptism, what I am calling "the deep well" and "the lively works" of Christian baptism. First, I want to go back to the beginning, to chart the flow of God's covenant designs as they are built upon creation. Far too briefly, I'll touch on a few crests or highpoints of redemptive history as it bears on baptism: (1) the creation of the world, (2) the flood, (3) Israel's crossing of the Red Sea, (4) the priestly washing of Aaron and his sons, all of which leads to (5) the culmination of the new covenant and Christ's institution of water baptism.

Then, second, having ascended the mountainside, we will refresh ourselves by looking at baptism's lively works. Drawing from our Old Testament study, we will ask the question, What exactly does baptism do? Or, better said, What exactly does *God* do in new covenant baptism? My hope is that, through this study, you and I would marvel at God's good gift in baptism, and that our marveling would strengthen our trust in the Christ who commanded baptism to be properly observed and profoundly cherished in the church he loves.

The Deep Well of Christian Baptism

What is the deep well of new covenant baptism? From what does it spring? In his study of the sacramental theology of the early church, Jean Daniélou writes, "If we wish to understand the true meaning of Baptism, it is quite clear that we must turn to the Old Testament."[1]

---

1. Jean Daniélou, SJ, *The Bible and the Liturgy* (Notre Dame, IN: University of Notre Dame Press, 1956), 71.

The Waters of Creation

The first Old Testament hint, the first deep background to baptism, is the primal waters of the original creation. I am not saying that the original creation was a baptism, and I realize that even a connection between God's original creation and new covenant baptism might seem tenuous. The Latin father Jerome probably goes too far when he describes the Holy Spirit's bringing forth the world from water as "a type of the Christian child that is drawn from the laver of baptism."[2] But the parallels between creation and water baptism are striking. After God creates the world out of water and through water, he consecrates this world to himself, ushers it into covenant, and promises blessing. Along the way, he issues a threefold blessing: one for birds and fish to multiply (Gen. 1:22), another for mankind to be fruitful and fill the earth (Gen. 1:28), and another blessing on the seventh day of his Sabbath rest (Gen. 2:3). Out of the waters of baptism, too, God promises to bless. He promises to bless all who flee to Christ through faith. He promises to build his church. And he promises the Holy Spirit to all whom he has chosen, that through Christ they might drink deeply of "the river of the water of life, bright as crystal, flowing from the throne of God and of the Lamb" (Rev. 22:1).

But let us not get ahead of ourselves. As Old Testament history advances, the Spirit's hovering over those primal waters of the first creation gives way to two further events that echo dimensions of the creation event and that Scripture *explicitly*

---

2. Jerome, "The Letters of St. Jerome," in *St. Jerome: Letters and Select Works*, ed. Philip Schaff and Henry Wace, trans. W. H. Fremantle, G. Lewis, and W. G. Martley, vol. 6, *A Select Library of the Nicene and Post-Nicene Fathers of the Christian Church*, Second Series (New York: Christian Literature Company, 1893), 145.

identifies as baptisms—namely, the global flood and Israel's crossing of the Red Sea, each a covenantal transaction that marked a new creational beginning.

The Flood of Noah's Day

Consider first the flood in Noah's day. This event proved that the same waters from which God first created life also harbored the power of death. In the beginning, God twice parted the original waters of the earth, separating the waters below from those above and then separating the waters below to make land appear (Gen. 1:7, 9). In the flood, he does the reverse, bursting the fountains of the deep and opening the windows of heaven (Gen. 7:11) to cover the earth and its every inhabitant on account of the extreme wickedness of human sin (Gen. 6:5–7).

Yet, in bringing death, the flood waters also cleared the way for a redemptive rebirth of creation itself. It is no wonder that Tertullian calls the flood "the baptism of the world."[3] To use Peter's words, the deluge marked a transition in history from "the world that then existed," drowned in death, to the rising up of "the heavens and the earth that now exist" (2 Pet. 3:6–7). Taken as a whole, the flood was a new creation event, reminiscent of the first creation. God caused his "wind" (רוח; *rûaḥ*) to blow over the subsiding waters (Gen. 8:1), recalling the Spirit's hovering over the original creation. Three times a dove surveyed the reemerging land (Gen. 8:8–12), recalling the land's original appearance on the third day of the creation

---

3. Tertullian, "On Baptism," in *Latin Christianity: Its Founder, Tertullian*, ed. Alexander Roberts, James Donaldson, and A. Cleveland Coxe, trans. S. Thelwall, vol. 3, The Ante-Nicene Fathers (Buffalo, NY: Christian Literature Company, 1885), 673.

week (Gen. 1:9–12). Finally, the array of animals that trot, crawl, and fly out of the ark to be fruitful and multiply (Gen. 8:17) emulated God's creating and loosing just such an array on the fifth day of creation (Gen. 1:20–25).

One key difference is that unlike Adam, Noah ("a righteous man" [Gen. 6:9]), obeyed the Lord and broke through the world's watery grave to ascend the mountain of God as the representative of a new humanity.[4] Noah's sacrifices from among the animals under his dominion (Gen. 8:20) pleased God's nostrils, and so foreshadowed the future consummation of the covenant of grace, when the one greater than Noah will usher his redeemed church into a recreated cosmos "after destroying every rule and every authority and power" (1 Cor. 15:24; cf. Matt. 24:38–39).

Oh, we could linger here for a while! But let us simply point out how in a similar way, in baptism, every baptized person formally enters the new covenant community of the church, the visible firstfruits of God's new creation in Christ. Of course, water baptism does not guarantee salvation to its every recipient, no more than Noah's ark guaranteed Ham's reconciliation to God. Nevertheless, water baptism pictures Paul's declaration to the Corinthians that "if anyone is in Christ, he is a new creation. The old has passed away; behold, the new has come" (2 Cor. 5:17). Peter explicitly says that Noah's ark-deliverance through the flood finds an explicit New Testament analog in water baptism. Just as "a few, that is, eight persons, were brought safely through water," he explains, so "baptism, which corresponds to this, now saves you" (1 Pet.

---

4. See G. K. Beale, *A New Testament Biblical Theology: The Unfolding of the Old Testament in the New* (Grand Rapids, MI: Baker, 2011), 413.

3:20–21a). Peter's strong sacramental language does not mean that God's sanctifying grace is inherent within the sacrament as it works *ex opere operato* (by the work worked). Rather, he means that just as the flood waters "saved" Noah and his family by floating them to safety, so in baptism the Holy Spirit consecrates the baptized in the new covenant, where God will save them if they believe on Christ.

In water baptism today, every baptized person passes through a mini-flood. Every time a minister baptizes, God recapitulates the promises, warnings, privileges, and obligations that Noah and his household received so long ago. Speaking of that warning, if a person rejects the blessing that baptism signifies, those baptismal waters will rise up, as it were, in the eschatological flood on the last day to consign that soul to a baptism of fire that will consume the unbelieving world (2 Pet. 3:6–7, 10). "For as were the days of Noah," Jesus says, "so will be the coming of the Son of Man" (Matt. 24:37). On that day, God will relegate his enemies to the deep. But also, gloriously, he will purify the elect as they enter into his heavenly presence in a renewed cosmos (see Matt. 13:47–50; Rev. 20:15).

Israel's Exodus through the Red Sea

What about Israel's Red Sea crossing? Here the waters performed dual covenantal functions a second time. On the one hand, God defeated Pharoah by immersing Israel's Egyptian pursuers unto death (Ex. 14:27–28). To use prophetic language, God slayed Rahab, the sea-monster that symbolized Egypt (Isa. 51:9–10). On the other hand, God liberated Israel from slavery for the purpose of worship and communion with himself by passage through the same waters. Just as Noah's ark landed on a mountain where he could offer sacrifice to God, so in the exodus God funneled his people through the sea to his holy mountain at Sinai, and eventually to Mount Zion in Jerusalem (Ex. 15:17), that they might serve him.[5] Looking back, one can see how, in a kind of corporate baptism, God was washing Israel and beckoning them all—parents and their children—out of servitude to sin and into worship of his name.

God does the same thing in new covenant baptism. He consecrates parents and their children to himself and calls them to the privileges and responsibilities of covenant life in the church. Like the split sea that Israel traversed, baptism exemplifies a channel of escape from slavery to sin into freedom in Christ (Rom. 6:3–4, 17–23). Just as Israel passed through the waters to become a kingdom of priests and a holy nation (Ex. 19:4–6), so, too, in baptism one is brought into membership in God's expanded and sanctified covenant community—God's "holy nation" (1 Pet. 2:9)—on this side of the cross. Those who break covenant by profaning the blood and water that flowed from Christ's side will join Satan's legions in the lake of fire (cf. Heb. 10:28; Rev. 20:15). But those who fulfill their baptismal contract with genuine faith will "sing the song of Moses . . . and the song of the Lamb" (Rev. 15:3) as they stand, victorious, by the sea of glass, having conquered the beast by abiding in the Savior to the end.[6]

Allow me to make one more point about this Old Testament redemption. The New Testament teaches that Israel's passage

---

5. On the theme of deliverance unto worship in the presence of Yahweh as structuring the Pentateuch as a whole, with the day of atonement in Leviticus at its center, see L. Michael Morales, *Who Shall Ascend the Mountain of the Lord? A Biblical Theology of the Book of Leviticus*, New Studies in Biblical Theology (Downers Grove, IL: InterVarsity, 2015), 23–38.

6. G. K. Beale, *The Book of Revelation: A Commentary on the Greek Text*, NIGTC (Grand Rapids, MI: Eerdmans, 1999), 792.

through the Sea was not just a picture of water baptism, it was a baptism in its own right. Looking back, Paul writes, "all were baptized into Moses in the cloud and in the sea" (1 Cor. 10:2), just as they "all ate the same spiritual food, and all drank the same spiritual drink" (vv. 3–4a). In doing so, "they drank from the spiritual Rock that followed them, and the Rock was Christ" (v. 4b).

With these words Paul pushes us to remember that the major Old Testament events like the exodus were not simply bare analogies to new covenant realities. They were true administrations of God's one covenant of grace. Even in the Old Testament period, Israel had no other effective mediator but Christ. As Vos writes, by the power of Christ's eternal anointing "He already exercised His threefold office through the service of the shadows."[7] As Moses led the whole nation out of Pharaoh's coils, and as the nation trusted in Moses as God's man (see Ex. 14:31), God vividly signified and sealed their status as his covenant people under none other than Christ. God baptized both them and their children through the water of the Red Sea in the name of Christ and called them to faith and obedience in Christ. And by traversing between the sea's watery walls (v. 22), the Israelites swore their allegiance to Moses as Christ's chosen "shadow," under the aegis of their covenant-making and covenant-keeping Lord and Messiah to come.

The shadows may be gone, but water baptism signifies the same obligation, urges the same endurance, and manifests the same declaration of allegiance as Israel experienced—an allegiance we give not to Moses, but to Christ himself, now cru-

---

7. Vos, *Reformed Dogmatics*, 3:11.

cified and raised! In other words, water baptism today warns of the same divine judgment and harbors the same heavenly blessing as did Israel's exodus-baptism. Only it does all of this for a people who live at a later stage of redemptive history, on this side of the cross, and who, therefore, should respond to the call of baptism much better than did the baptized Israelites of old.

Aaron's Ordination to the Priesthood

One final Old Testament precursor informs new covenant baptism, and to an unusual degree. It is the rite of ordination for Aaron and his sons to the priesthood (Exodus 29; Leviticus 8). The symbolism of this ordination process reaches back to creation, echoing Adam's calling as the first priest in the earthly courts of God. It picks up the later history of Israel, too, as its ritual sacrificing (Ex. 29:10–20), blood smearing (vv. 12, 20), and eating of holy meat (vv. 28, 32–33) replicates the Passover celebration and reflects Israel's corporate calling as a nation of priests to God. But as it bears on water baptism today, of particular interest in Aaron's ordination is God's command to Moses at the beginning of the ceremony, "You shall bring Aaron and his sons to the entrance of the tent of meeting and wash them with water" (v. 4; cf. Lev. 8:6).

At least three elements regarding this command interestingly dovetail with new covenant baptism.[8] First, this was the only water ritual in the Old Testament in which one person

---

8. While the explanations are my own, I owe attention to these points to Isaac Augustine Morales, OP, *The Bible and Baptism: The Fountain of Salvation* (Grand Rapids, MI: Baker Academic, 2022), 71, who cites Peter J. Leithart, *The Priesthood of the Plebs: A Theology of Baptism* (Eugene, OR: Wipf & Stock, 2003), 95–96.

washed another (Lev. 8:6).[9] Second, the washing of Aaron and his sons was the only Old Testament purification ritual that took place only once. This is because the washing signified an induction to office. Fittingly, it took place at "the entrance of the tent of meeting" (Ex. 29:4), where Israel's high priests were called to serve. Third, after being washed, Aaron and his sons were clothed in special priestly garments (vv. 5–9). These garments, originally designed "for glory and beauty" (Ex. 28:40), replicated the divine glory and beauty that God promised would one day clothe all of his people (see Isa. 28:5).

Baptism today replicates these features of Aaron's washing in the new covenant era. First, baptism consecrates its recipients for fellowship with God in temple service in the church. But whereas in the Old Testament only Aaron and his sons were set apart as high priests, today through baptism all professing believers and all their offspring are consecrated in Christ's kingdom (1 Pet. 2:4–5). And when and as they believe on Christ, they do not enjoy merely provisional and indirect access to God through an earthly veil, but more direct and continual access to God's heavenly sanctuary through Christ's blood.

In fact, the author of Hebrews draws on Aaron and his sons' ordination to the priesthood when it reminds us of our "confidence to enter the holy places by the blood of Jesus" (Heb.

---

9. The only other administered washing was the sprinkling of the Levites (Num. 8:5–7), a similar ceremony of dedication to sanctuary service. One difference is that while the Levites are brought into the sphere of the ritually clean (טָהֹר; *ṭāhôr*) to support tabernacle and temple worship, the priests are brought into the sphere of the holy (קָדֹשׁ; *qādôš*) to handle the sacred objects themselves. Timothy R. Ashley, *The Book of Numbers*, NICOT (Grand Rapids, MI: Eerdmans, 1993), 169.

10:19).[10] The author goes on, "Let us draw near with a true heart in full assurance of faith, with our hearts sprinkled clean from an evil conscience and our bodies washed with pure water" (v. 22). Just as Aaron and his sons were sprinkled with blood, washed with water, and clothed in new vestments, so the outward sign of baptism symbolizes all three dimensions in their inward application through faith in Christ. In every baptism, the church beholds God's promise and power to purify the heart, to cleanse from sin, and to clothe the sinner in Christ's righteousness through faith.

Christ's "Baptisms"

All of these Old Testament "baptisms"—from creation to the flood, to Israel's exodus and Aaron's ordination—lead directly to Christ and his saving work. And there they split into four related channels: Jesus's water baptism by John in the Jordan river, Jesus's "baptism" in death on the cross, his messianic "Spirit-and-fire" baptism of the church at Pentecost, and, finally, his institution of covenant baptism for the church until he returns.

John's baptizing ministry signaled the final stage of God's covenant lawsuit against an unbelieving nation, a sort of "last call" for his hearers to turn from their sin and escape God's impending judgment.[11] But when Jesus himself came to John for baptism, he balked. What John found so startling, what explains his reluctance to baptize Jesus (see Matt. 3:14), and

---

10. Leithart, *The Priesthood of the Plebs*, 99–102; F. W. Flemington, *The New Testament Doctrine of Baptism* (London: SPCK, 1957), 98.
11. Meredith G. Kline, *By Oath Consigned: A Reinterpretation of the Covenant Sings of Circumcision and Baptism* (Grand Rapids, MI: Eerdmans, 1975), 51–55.

what gets to the heart of Jesus's eventual baptism by John is that God's blessing of salvation to Israel and the world would come about only because the Messiah would first, himself, undergo the divine curse symbolized in baptism.

Jesus spoke of his impending sufferings on the cross as "baptism" in Luke 12:50, declaring, "I have a baptism to be baptized with, and how great is my distress until it is accomplished!" Inasmuch as Jesus engaged in a lifelong ordeal against the powers of darkness in this sin-cursed world, and inasmuch as his whole earthly life was a test of his sinless obedience, his entire ministry on earth was "a species of baptism."[12] But Jesus's words in Luke 12:50 have particular reference to the cross, where he endured a baptismal judgment of eschatological proportions. On the cross Jesus removed God's curse from every sinner who hopes in him in order to deliver them, Noah-like and Moses-like, into the imperishable land of heaven. Moreover, by his baptism on the cross, Christ heralded God's righteousness far more solemnly than Noah did, and he accomplished an exodus far greater than Moses led through the Red Sea. And his cross-work conveys real power to Christians today. For example, when Paul declares that "all of us who have been baptized into Christ Jesus were baptized into his death" (Rom. 6:3) so that "we too might walk in newness of life" (v. 4), he means that the new life God communicates in baptism through faith arises out of what has taken place in Christ's death and resurrection.[13]

Of course, Jesus communicates this life to Christians today

---

12. Richard B. Gaffin Jr., *In the Fullness of Time: An Introduction to the Biblical Theology of Acts and Paul* (Wheaton, IL: Crossway, 2022), 117.

13. Herman Ridderbos, *Paul: An Outline of His Theology*, trans. John R. De Witt (Grand Rapids, MI: Eerdmans, 1975), 213.

through the Holy Spirit, with whom he baptized the household of the church on the day of Pentecost. Even so, let us never lose sight of the eschatological significance of that historical event. As Gaffin observes, "Pentecost is part of the end-time judicial transaction of God. It is of a piece with God's eschatological adjudication."[14] That is, the Spirit of Pentecost falls on the church as a tidal wave of eschatological judgment-discrimination. How so? It is by the Spirit that God bestows his favor upon the repentant "wheat" and seals his judgment upon the ultimately unrepentant "chaff" Until Christ's return. The Spirit does this very work by progressively showering Christ's riches on the elect, even as he "convict[s] the world concerning sin and righteousness and judgment" (John 16:8) for its rejection of Christ. In all this, the Spirit uses the Word preached. But he also uses baptism, and the Lord's Supper. For its part, baptism is like a battle flag planted into the ground, an emblem of Christ, to whom the elect flee for refuge and from whom the reprobate try in vain to evade as the final day draws near.

Alas, our survey of the deep waters of covenant baptism is far too shallow. But we need to turn now to the other side of this world of theology. Following the great fountain of God's mercy as it rises up in the new covenant in Christ, let us ask the all-important question: What exactly does baptism do today?

The Lively Works of Christian Baptism

As we gather up God's baptismal dealings with his people and see them funneled into this simple sacrament, I believe we find water baptism doing at least seven things. Baptism signifies, summons, seals, sanctifies, sets apart, swears, and strengthens.

---

14. Gaffin, *In the Fullness of Time*, 100.

Baptism Signifies

First, baptism *signifies* God's provision of salvation and the purifying power of new life in Christ. Baptism is one sign among many in covenant history. We can think, of course, of the rainbow in the sky (Gen. 9:12–16), the sign of circumcision (Gen. 17:11), the paschal lamb (Ex. 12:13–14), and the Sabbath day (Ex. 31:16–17).[15] But baptism shines especially bright in the history of redemption. For it signals what Jonah announced after God rescued him from a watery death, "Salvation belongs to the LORD" (Jonah 2:9). Baptism announces that the Father has given to Christ the power to save (Matt. 11:27; John 5:21–24). He is the one who is "greater than Jonah" (Matt. 12:41). He is the one who lifts sinners from death and initiates them into fellowship with him and with his Father in heaven (Eph. 2:18; 1 Pet. 3:18). Baptism signifies Christ's saving power for sinners, applied to them from heaven. Additionally, the waters poured over the head of the baptized also signify the effusion of the Spirit on the church for the saving, sanctifying, and sustaining of Christians in the safety of God's embrace. In short, baptism symbolizes God's salvation of sinners through Christ, particularly as Christ has poured out the Holy Spirit upon the church at Pentecost for the uniting of sinners in every age to himself according to his cleansing and purifying power.

But baptism signifies more. As the Old Testament flood and Israel's Red Sea crossing demonstrated in typical form, the same "good news" of the gospel—that Christ has endured God's wrath on behalf of all who trust in him—also indirectly warns of the "bad news" of judgment when God's wrath will

---

15. Cf. Sinclair Ferguson, "Infant Baptism View," in *Baptism: Three Views*, ed. David F. Wright (Downers Grove, IL: InterVarsity, 2009), 85.

fall upon all who are not united to Christ (John 3:36), and even more upon those who tragically refuse to believe on Christ despite their being baptized (Matt. 7:21–23).[16] Because baptism signifies this full gospel, it is as symbolically redolent with the judgment, condemnation, and death that Christ has endured and will one day administer as Judge (Matt. 25:31–46; Acts 17:31; 2 Cor. 5:10) as it is with the trustworthy hope of salvation unto eternal life through him as the only Savior. No wonder John the Baptist announced that Jesus would baptize "with the Holy Spirit and with fire" (Luke 3:16).

Scripture teaches that the Spirit works like fire. Fire kindles to destroy as well as cleanses to renew (see Isa. 4:4; 30:33; Luke 3:16–17; John 16:8–11). Similarly, water energizes but also devours as a deluge (see Ps. 42:7; 88:7; Mic. 1:4; Matt. 24:38–39; Titus 3:5–6). Both functions are bound up in John the Baptist's prediction about Christ's baptizing work. His baptism with the Spirit was and remains a great discriminating work, yielding blessing for the repentant and destruction for the unrepentant.[17] So, too, in its signifying function, water baptism pictures the Holy Spirit's activity to save *and* to judge—to cleanse *and* to consume.

Baptism Summons

Second, baptism *summons*. As a sign, it summons sinners to receive the salvation that it symbolizes. As circumcision did for the adult Jew and his male offspring, baptism, too, urges a

---

16. Citing John 4:1–2 and 6:36, Zwingli notes that through his disciples (John 4:1–2), Jesus baptized many who did not believe at the time. Huldrych Zwingli, "Of Baptism," in *Zwingli and Bullinger*, trans. G. W. Bromiley (Philadelphia, PA: Westminster, 1952), 135.

17. Gaffin, *In the Fullness of Time*, 104.

response to the gospel it depicts. As a green light at an intersection instructs drivers to press forward, or like a masterpiece painting commands the heart's attention, baptism urges the baptized to exercise saving faith in Christ and to manifest such faith through Spirit-wrought works of obedience. Baptism also warns the baptized to flee from the flood of wrath that awaits those who fail to heed the water's command to lay hold of Christ through faith (Col. 3:3; Rev. 6:16). In the case of professing adults, the summons of baptism encourages them to ensure they have believed on Christ and are walking in step with his Spirit (Rom. 8:4; Gal. 5:16). In the case of young children growing towards spiritual birth and maturity, baptism's summons invites them to appropriate for themselves all that their baptism signifies, as we pray that they will do while faithful parents and churches rear them in the love, discipline, and instruction of the Lord, including by teaching covenant children what their baptism means (Eph. 6:4).

Baptism Seals

Third, the sacrament of baptism that signifies and summons also *seals*, or confirms, the validity of God's promise of salvation in Christ. That is, God not only instructs the baptized by bringing to mind what baptism signifies, and he not only summons the baptized to Christ and to faith-fueled new obedience, but he also confirms to them and to all the witnessing church the reliability of his promise to save through faith in Christ. Like circumcision in the Old Testament, baptism is a stamp of authenticity, a mark of divine approval, of God's sovereign promise to redeem a people for himself. Today, just as the Word preached conveys the promise of the gospel to the ear, so baptism confirms to the eye God's declaration of saving grace to all who believe, assuring everyone of God's willingness to give such faith according to his good pleasure.

Baptism seals objectively (in the sense that it "guarantees") to our hearts God's inviolable promise to save sinners through faith in Christ and, by implication, to judge those who are baptized with water (or who are never baptized at all) but never come to faith in Christ (Matt. 7:21–23; Rev. 20:14–15; cf. Ezek. 26:19; Nah. 1:8; Hos. 5:10). From this perspective, baptism is a seal to every baptized person, to every eyewitness in the church, and even to every sinner in the world. But baptism also seals subjectively—that is, baptism "assures a partaking of"—God's salvation to those baptized individuals who have genuinely believed, or else who will believe, on Christ. From this perspective, baptism as a seal of the invisible benefits of redemption affixes those benefits upon those to whom, by God's grace, those benefits belong.

In these ways, baptism's sealing function supports weak faith by assuring the church that the salvation portrayed in the sacrament will be realized according to God's plan, in God's time, and by God's power. It confirms to the recipient open access to the riches of Christ. In short, baptism's seal character guarantees God's special care for those who confess the name of Christ and, as we will see more explicitly below, for their children, as well (Isa. 44:3; Jer. 31:36; Matt. 19:13–14; Acts 2:39; 1 Cor. 7:14; Eph. 6:1).

Baptism Sanctifies

Fourth, as baptism seals, or confirms, God's promise to save his own, through baptism God also *sanctifies* those whom he chooses. Baptism is a "means of grace."[18] The Bible teaches that when God calls the elect to faith and new obedience in Christ, he does not leave them alone in responding but grants to them the gift of faith and repentance unto life (Acts 11:18; Eph. 2:8–9; 2 Tim. 2:25) and impels their obedience by his indwelling Spirit (Rom. 8:4; 1 Cor. 12:6; 15:10; Phil. 2:13; 2 Thess. 1:11; Heb. 13:21). In other words, as God issues the call to faith and looks for its fruits (signifying and summoning), as God guarantees saving power in the sign he gives (sealing), he also gives the faith he demands and grows the fruit he desires in those whom he will (Hos. 14:8; John 15:5).

God normally performs this extraordinary work by means of the preached Word, for "faith comes from hearing, and hearing through the word of Christ" (Rom. 10:17). But Scripture and the Reformed tradition teach that God has always strengthened his people through all of his ordained means of grace, including baptism. As believers "improve" their baptism—that is, consciously draw upon the promises and benefits of baptism—as the Westminster Divines put it,[19] God

---

18. Berkhof helpfully describes God's means of grace as "objective channels which Christ has instituted in the Church, and to which He ordinarily binds Himself in the communication of His grace." Louis Berkhof, *Systematic Theology* (Grand Rapids, MI: Eerdmans, 1938), 604–605.

19. See WLC 167: "Q. *How is our baptism to be improved by us?* A. The needful but much neglected duty of improving our baptism, is to be performed by us all our life long, especially in the time of temptation, and when we are present at the administration of it to others; by serious and thankful consideration of the nature of it, and of the ends for which Christ instituted it, the privileges and benefits conferred and sealed thereby, and our solemn vow made therein; by being humbled for our sinful defilement, our falling short of, and walking contrary to, the grace of baptism, and our engagements; by growing up to assurance of pardon of sin, and of all other blessings sealed to us in that sacrament; by drawing strength from the death and resurrection of Christ, into whom we are baptized, for the mortifying of

increases the faith by which his people lay hold on Christ and obey him as he speaks in Scripture. Baptism steadies the trembling hearts that receive Christ as he is offered in the gospel. The waters of baptism signify redemptive grace that may seem slow in coming, even long after someone is baptized. But as the Spirit finally breaks a stony heart through years of preaching, the grace conveyed in baptism may at last saturate a needy soul and nourish new obedience. As the Belgic Confession (Art. 33) declares, the sacraments are "visible signs and seals of an inward and invisible thing, *by means whereof* God works in us by the power of the Holy Spirit. Therefore the signs are not empty or meaningless, so as to deceive us."[20]

God can do his sanctifying work the moment the water is administered, even prior to it (see Luke 1:15, 44; Acts 10:47–48), or long after someone is baptized. But when and where he determines, and to whom he chooses, God uses baptism to elicit or to strengthen the faith the sacrament calls for and to enable the faith-fueled obedience baptism demands.[21]

---

sin, and quickening of grace; and by endeavoring to live by faith, to have our conversation in holiness and righteousness, as those that have therein given up their names to Christ; and to walk in brotherly love, as being baptized by the same Spirit into one body."

20. James T. Dennison Jr., *Reformed Confessions of the 16th and 17th Centuries in English Translation: 1523–1693*, 2 vols. (Grand Rapids, MI: Reformation Heritage Books, 2008–2014), 2:444. Emphasis added.

21. This point is helpfully enshrined in WCF 28.6: "The efficacy of baptism is not tied to that moment of time wherein it is administered; yet, notwithstanding, by the right use of this ordinance, the grace promised is not only offered, but really exhibited, and conferred, by the Holy Ghost, to such (whether of age or infants) as that grace belongeth unto, according to the counsel of God's own will, in his appointed time."

Baptism Sets Apart

Fifth, through baptism God visibly *sets apart* a people for himself. As was the case with circumcision in the Old Testament period, the sacrament of baptism is not to be applied to everyone but only to those whom God brings under the aegis of Christ's redemptive Lordship as members of his covenant community. To put it in terms of Jesus's institution of baptism in the Great Commission, baptism is for those who are genuinely his disciples. But just who are they?

In the case of adults, their discipleship is marked by Spirit-wrought faith expressed in a credible profession (2 Cor. 4:13). To be specific, saving faith is a prerequisite for the baptism of an adult, hence the church baptizes an adult on the basis of the closest thing to that reality—namely, his or her profession of repentance and faith in Christ (Luke 3:8; John 15:8).

But adults are not the only people capable of becoming disciples under of the reign of King Jesus. Given Old Testament precedent from the beginning of covenant history, children, too, are to be received into his organized and discipling church. Jesus demonstrated this when believing parents brought their children—"even infants" (Luke 18:15)—to be blessed by him. When his disciples resisted their approach, the Lord answered, "Let the children come to me, and do not hinder them, for to such belongs the kingdom of God" (v. 16; cf. Matt. 19:14; Mark 10:14). Jesus's point was not that the kingdom of God belongs to all children, but that the children who are deliberately brought to him for his blessing fall under the discipling power of his kingdom. Luke tells us, "Now they [that is, parents, especially, fathers, given the masculine Greek pronoun] were bringing even infants to him" (Luke 18:15). By laying his hands upon these children (see Mark 10:16), Jesus affirmed their privilege of participating in his kingdom, the church.

Today, the children of believing parents still occupy a definite place in the administration of his kingdom, which comes to visible expression in Christ's organized church on earth (Matt. 16:18–19). And because baptism visibly consecrates disciples to Christ in his church, one can begin to see how the sacrament of baptism rightly sets apart the children of professing Christians along with their parents. While God always retains the prerogative to inwardly call and convert any whom he will—"everyone whom the Lord our God calls to himself"—God still declares to professing Jews and Gentiles that the "promise is for you and for your children" (Acts 2:39).

Baptism Swears

Sixth, part of the Lord's design for baptism is that it might serve as a means by which church members *swear* back to him their commitment to him for faith and obedience. Careful readers will note how all of the previous functions of baptism run from God to the baptized recipient. But this function runs from the recipient back to God! Here is a good place to remember that, in its ancient usage, the Latin word *sacramentum* designated the oath by which Roman soldiers swore their fidelity to their general and to one another.[22] In a similar way, as with circumcision in the Old Testament, those who submit to the sacrament of baptism symbolically enter into a sworn covenant with God. By baptism, one is sworn to the triune God, dedicated to the Father according to his electing love, through the sanctifying work of the Spirit, for obedience to

---

22. Daniel G. Van Slyke, "The Changing Meanings of *sacramentum*: Historical Sketches," *Antiphon* 11.3 (2007): 247.

Jesus Christ in a bond of fellowship that is sealed by his sprinkled blood (1 Pet. 1:2).

In the case of young children, the swearing dimension of their baptism runs through their parents, who swear their commitment to raise their little ones to know and serve the Lord. No doubt many here made such a vow as you held your baby out towards the waters. There is a unique bond between parent and child. It bends but does not break. Many Christian wives are helpless to bring their unbelieving husbands to church. But they are able and authorized by God to bring their children to church, where they will be instructed to "obey your parents in the Lord" (Eph. 6:1). A Christian husband may pray for the conversion of his unbelieving wife. But regardless of her unbelief, God calls him to raise his children "in the discipline and instruction of the Lord" (v. 4). Likewise, Paul declares that the children of a believing parent are not "unclean" but "holy" (1 Cor. 7:14)—that is, divinely set apart from all other children of the world and privileged to live within a familial bond, a bond poised to mediate God's saving grace to them (Mark 10:13; 1 Thess. 2:11; cf. Deut. 11:19; Ps. 78:4; Joel 1:3).

In baptism, God visibly expresses his proprietary interest in the recipients, his gracious provisions for them, and what he expects from them. And in baptism, the baptized yield to it all. For them, baptism ratifies not only an offer that should be accepted (for the preaching of the gospel does as much as this), but also an acquiescence on the part of the baptized to exhibit repentance and faith in Christ in due time. In other words, God enhances the summons of baptism for all whom he sets apart, especially the children of believers, by placing upon them a unique and special responsibility to come to the

Savior signified in their baptism. The circumcision of Israel's male children involved them in the same spiritual oath of discipleship (Gen. 17:9–14; Jer. 4:4; cf. Deut. 29:10–13) before Christ's incarnation, and the same incumbency is true today for believers and their offspring who are baptized in the wake of Christ's ascension.[23]

Baptism Strengthens

Finally, baptism *strengthens* the bonds among those who belong to the church, God's covenant community under Christ. Many who have witnessed a typical infant baptism in their churches will attest to the unifying power of the rite. When the time comes for a child to be baptized, it is common for the child's parents to "promise, in humble reliance upon divine grace," to raise their son or daughter "in the nurture and admonition of the Lord."[24] But often the pastor will then ask the congregation, "Do you as a congregation undertake the responsibility of assisting the parents in the Christian nurture of this child?"[25] The collective, positive, and often audible response of the visible body of Christ inevitably buoys the parents' souls and tangibly expresses the church's commitment to "maintain the unity of the Spirit in the bond of peace" (Eph. 4:3). Similarly, when an adult is baptized after a profession of faith, the collective prayers of the church ascend to God, as hearts and even hands (!) reach out to embrace the new covenant member in love. In each case, the divine power and grace

---

23. As the WSC 94 notes, in the case of an adult or child, baptism signifies and seals an "engagement to be the Lord's."
24. *The Book of Church Order of the Presbyterian Church in America* (Lawrenceville, GA: The Office of the Stated Clerk of the General Assembly of the Presbyterian Church in America, 2023), 56–5.
25. *The Book of Church Order of the Presbyterian Church in America*, 56–5.

signified and expressed in a water baptism ripple through the congregation that looks on together in faith.

Conclusion: Countless Blessings

So, there you have it. Out of the deep well of covenant history, baptism pours forth countless blessings upon the church. Through baptism God *signifies* the gospel, *summons* the baptized to faith, *seals* his covenant promises, objectively to the church and to the world, and subjectively to the elect. As baptism confirms the Word that begets faith, through baptism God *sanctifying* his elect. In baptism, God sets apart his visible church from the world, as they in turn *swear* themselves back to God. And in baptism, God *strengthens* the fellowship of his people, one with one another, in the Spirit poured out upon the church.

Like a torrential river channeled into a tiny rivulet, God channels the richness of his covenant purposes into the simple sacrament of water baptism. Building on creation, the flood, the Red Sea crossing, Aaron's priestly ordination, and more Old Testament washings, water baptism is a key instrument of Christ's heavenly ministry, the visible act that represents who he is, all he has done, and all he will do as the Messiah.

Because the blessings of baptism are so glorious, they ought to be understood, treasured, and proclaimed by all who belong to Christ. Far more abundantly than that mountain spring in North Carolina, may the Lord use baptism to enrich the church united to Jesus Christ. And in her baptizing ministry, may the church cherish the new covenant blessings that belong to us and to our children forever. For Christ belongs to us, and we to him, and he is with us until the end of the age. Praise the Lord that all who are baptized into his death and resurrection through faith will be with him into the endless consummation to come, when we will thirst no more.

6

THE CHURCH'S MISSION IS TEACHING

Matthew 28:20a

JAMES J. CASSIDY

IN CHAPTER 2, I made the categorical statement that the work of the church is missions. Missions, I noted, is summed up by the biblical injunction: "preach the Word." Everything the church does is either preaching the gospel, serves preaching the gospel, or points to or flows from the gospel preached.

While the church engages in various activities such as administering sacraments, showing mercy, exercising church discipline, worshiping, and praying, all these things ultimately serve the mission of the church. For example, mercy allows preaching to go unhindered, prayer asks for God's kingdom to come through preaching, and the sacraments visibly portray the same gospel that is preached.

But what about teaching? The Bible instructs the church to teach, as evidenced by Jesus's command in the Great Commission. Teaching was the main activity of our Lord in the Gospels. Paul speaks about the church's "standard of teaching" (Rom. 6:17), and every believer is to hold fast to the apostolic teaching. Colossians 1:28 says that the apostolic task is to proclaim Christ, which includes warning and teaching everyone. Furthermore, believers are to let the Word of Christ dwell in them, admonishing and teaching one another with it (Col. 3:16). Timothy is exhorted to "devote yourself to the public reading of Scripture, to exhortation, to teaching" (1 Tim. 4:13). He is commanded to "keep a close watch on yourself and on the teaching" (v. 16). Paul commands sound teaching that "accords with godliness" (1 Tim. 6:3). And of course, the Great Commission contains the command to teach disciples to observe all things which Jesus commanded (Matt. 28:20).

Therefore, according to the Great Commission, the church's missional work *just is* teaching. I will seek to unpack that under three points:

1. Preaching and teaching are the same activity.
2. Jesus commands the church to declare the whole counsel of God.
3. Teaching *just is* the task of the church in the Great Commission.

Preaching and Teaching are the Same Activity

The relation between preaching and teaching has often been handled in a clumsy way. The real struggle has come with attempts to underscore the differences. In most cases, characteristics are assigned to each discipline that could just as readily be assigned to the other.

For example, one article at Logos says that what holds the two together is a common commitment to biblical and theological truth. The difference, it is claimed, is that preaching is the mode of invitation and exhortation, while teaching is concerned with explication and explanation.[1] However, preaching must also explain and explicate. After all, what are we doing in expository preaching if not explaining and explicating the meaning of the text? And would we ever want to say that our teaching may not have exhortation? After all, when Paul is instructing Timothy on sound teaching, he is doing it in the form of an exhortation! New Testament teaching is—dare I say—*always* hortatory.

Other descriptions of the differences abound. Even the best of them assign attributes to one discipline that—according to the Bible—can also be assigned to the other. Some propose differences that are grounded in contemporary experiences and observations. In other words, they are *descriptions* of modern phenomena rather than *prescriptions* that arise from Scripture. For example, some have described teaching as intellectual, seeking to reach the brain or mind, while preaching

---

1. James Pennington, "What's the Difference Between Preaching and Teaching?" (https://www.logos.com/grow/what-is-the-difference-between-preaching-and-teaching/#:~:text=We%20can%20define%20preaching%20as,goal%20of%20invitation%20and%20exhortation.) Accessed 18 August 2024.

is emotive, seeking to reach the heart. But this sounds like the description of someone who has experienced a lot of evangelical preaching, on the one hand, and lectures in today's institutes of higher learning, on the other.

The upshot of it all is that these proposed differences seem artificial. And at the end of the day, they are speculative because the Bible itself offers no technical difference. Furthermore, as we know, the same words in the Bible are often used in different ways, and sometimes different words in the Bible are used to communicate the same idea or reality.

I suspect that what is happening in the Great Commission is that the word *teaching* is used to describe the same activity that elsewhere in the Bible is designated as *preaching*. Let's consider some exegetical thoughts in support of this idea.

First, what does Jesus mean by "teaching them" (διδάσκω; *didaskō*) in Matthew 28:20a? It's impossible to come to a firm conclusion on lexical grounds alone. But we can get help from other parallel passages. We will consider texts from Luke and Acts, John, and Mark.

Luke 24:47 and Acts 1–2

The form of Luke 24:46–49 is not a commission, per se. Nevertheless, the substance of the commission in Matthew 28 is there, even though the wording is different: "and that repentance for the forgiveness of sins should be proclaimed in his name to all nations" (Luke 24:47). Instead of "make disciples" and "teaching them," Luke uses "be proclaimed." The word here is *kēryssō* (to herald or preach). So, the form and wording are different, but the substance is the same. We can draw a similar conclusion from Acts 1–2 where Luke continues his narrative from his Gospel. Acts 1:8, "you will be my witnesses in Jerusalem and in all Judea and Samaria, and to the end of the earth," substantially repeats Luke 24:47. The apostolic witness here is parallel to Luke 24:47, and the fourfold locus of that witness in Acts 1:8 parallels "all nations" in Luke 24:47. So, upon reception of the Holy Spirit in Acts 2, it is no surprise that the first activity we see is Peter preaching in Jerusalem.

The rest of Acts is about the preaching of the apostles. Here I would commend to you Dr. Gaffin's masterful biblical theology of Acts.[2] In short, he shows that Jesus's words about the apostolic witness from Jerusalem to Judea, Samaria, and the ends of the earth are fulfilled within Acts itself. There is no "Acts 29" where the church today fulfills the words of Jesus. That is not to say that we don't carry out the apostolic mission—we certainly do. Acts itself fulfills the fourfold progression of Jesus's commission, which serves as the book's framework. This progression begins with Peter's witness in Jerusalem, extends through Judea and Samaria, and culminates in Acts 28 with Paul "proclaiming (κήρυσσω; *kēryssō*) the kingdom of God and teaching about the Lord Jesus Christ with all boldness and without hindrance" (v. 31).

John 21:15–19

This is John's version of the Great Commission (sort of!). The context is the restoration of Peter. Peter's thrice denial of Jesus becomes a thrice adoration. In response, Jesus commands Peter to feed his sheep. This is the pastoral aspect of the apostolic ministry. Jesus here is commissioning not just Peter, but through Peter, all the apostles. Further, it should be noted, the

---

2. Richard B. Gaffin Jr., *In the Fullness of Time: An Introduction to the Biblical Theology of Acts and Paul* (Wheaton, IL: Crossway, 2022), 51–63.

pastoral ministry of the apostles is in imitation of the original shepherd himself. In John, the good shepherd's ministry is described as an oral ministry (John 10). His sheep listen to his voice (v. 16). Certainly, in verse 16, when Jesus speaks about "sheep that are not of this fold," he has in mind the mission to the Gentiles in the post-Pentecost period. Thus, the voice envisioned by Jesus in John 10 is his own ministry of Word and Spirit by means of the pastoral ministry of the apostles in which his sheep are fed. Of course, this happens through not only the apostles but also the subsequent ministers of the Word—a ministry that would continue to the end of the age (Matt. 28:20).

Further, we know this because of how Paul "hands off" the apostolic ministry to Timothy. The second generation of ministry also has its focus upon the preaching of the Word. We see this, for instance, in 1 Timothy 2:7, "For this I was appointed a preacher and an apostle (I am telling the truth, I am not lying), a teacher of the Gentiles in faith and truth." Note Paul's self-description. He was appointed as a *preacher*. But he then qualifies his ministry, using a synonym. As a preacher, he is a *teacher* of the Gentiles. He is an apostle who labors to fulfill the Great Commission to the nations, making them disciples by teaching them—that is, to preach to them.

This idea is repeated in 2 Timothy 1:11, "for which I was appointed a preacher and apostle and teacher." Paul also says more of the same in 1 Timothy 5:17, "Let the elders who rule well be considered worthy of double honor, especially those who labor in preaching and teaching." The Greek reads literally "labour in the word and doctrine" (KJV). The ESV rightly recognizes that "labour in the word and doctrine" are not two different activities, as if laboring in the word is one thing and doctrine is something else. Rather, the labor in view is singular. Further, the subject matter—the Word—is one. To "labour in the word" is a phrase meaning "preaching." And "doctrine" simply means "the teaching" which is taught from the Word.

He continues the prescription for post-apostolic ministry in 2 Timothy 4:2, "preach the word; be ready in season and out of season; reprove, rebuke, and exhort, with complete patience and teaching." We see again the connection between preaching and teaching. Timothy is to "preach the word." That preaching work includes reproving, rebuking, and exhorting, and is to be done with patience and teaching. Teaching here is in closest relation to preaching. In fact, we can say that the teaching *just is* the preaching. These are not two different activities but two different words describing one activity.

Mark 16:15

I am fully aware that this verse is in the extended version of Mark. I am not going to argue for the Textus Receptus: I think that Mark 6:9–20 are not canonical. But the parallel of Mark 16:15 to the Great Commission sheds light on the meaning of "teaching" in Matthew 28:20. While Mark 16:15 is not an infallible text, it can serve as a helpful guide. The verse reads: "Go into all the world and proclaim the gospel to the whole creation." Unlike in Luke, this is in the form of a commission. The apostles are to go and proclaim. Again, the word here is *kēryssō*. There are two differences with Matthew to note. First, instead of "all nations," Mark says, "whole creation." Certainly, these are synonyms. Second, Matthew's commission does not say preaching but rather "teaching." Yet Mark does use the language of "proclaim," or preach. Clearly, the author of the extended version of Mark uses "proclaim" as a synonym for *teaching.*

Given these parallel texts to the Great Commission of Matthew 28, we can rightly conclude that what Matthew has in mind when he records Jesus's command to teach *just is* the church's activity of preaching.

Jesus Commands the Church to Declare the Whole Counsel of God

The commission to make disciples by teaching them has at least three implications. First, preaching must be biblical-theological. Second, preaching must be systematic. Third, preaching must be polemical.

Preaching Must Be Biblical-Theological

Commentators on Matthew 28:20 are in basic agreement. The commentators recognize that this instruction to teach included broader subject matter than just the imperatives of Jesus. It is not as if the apostles are to only tell disciples what to do. It certainly includes that, but it includes more than that. The apostles are to teach disciples to obey—to believe and do—everything Jesus has commanded them to believe and to do. That includes not only imperative statements but also indicatives. It includes both doctrine and life.

Further, we know that Jesus's teachings are not contained only in what he said during the years 0–33 AD. According to Luke 24, everything in the Old Testament is a revelation of Jesus: "And beginning with Moses and all the Prophets, he interpreted to them in all the Scriptures the things concerning himself" (v. 27). Therefore, the teaching ministry of the church, as it seeks to make disciples—to gather and perfect the saints—is a ministry whereby disciples are taught everything revealed about Jesus from Genesis to Revelation. The history of special revelation—Genesis to Revelation—is the unfolding of the revelation of Jesus Christ, the Son of God. The disciple-making ministry of the church, as she seeks to proclaim the whole counsel of God, is to make Christ known. Him we proclaim, that we might present everyone mature in Christ (Col. 1:28)!

Preaching Must Be Systematic

Making known all that Christ has commanded—all of who he is, all of what he has done, all of his holy will for our lives—and faithfully proclaiming the whole counsel of God, means presenting the record of the history of special revelation in a clear, organized, coherent way. This is the task of systematic theology. And systematic theology is most necessary. For biblical theology without systematic theology is blind, just as systematic theology without biblical theology is empty. In the teaching ministry of the church, biblical theology and systematic theology are mutually dependent.

This is not to say that we preach systematic theology (though that is not illegitimate). But we do preach systematically. We preach in a way that teaches a text in light of all the other texts in biblical revelation. This necessarily means that our preaching is not to be biblicistic. Biblicistic preaching is atomistic preaching—that is, preaching a text in such a way that the text being preached is isolated. In biblicistic interpretation, the text is not informed by other texts or by our understanding of the whole body of theology.

While systematically preaching, we read a passage and abstract the event, or the action of a biblical character, from the rest of the context of the history of special revelation, whereas biblicistic preaching then makes that event, or action, a paradigm with universal application.

- Event A occurred under circumstance B; therefore, given any circumstance B, event A will (or should) occur.
- Character A took action B in circumstance C; therefore, given any circumstance C, we should take action B.
- God gives command A at historical time B; therefore, given any historical time, command A applies.

Regarding that third example, not all law is universal. Moral law is universal. But even the Ten Commandments (Ex. 20:1–17; Deut. 5:6–21), in terms of its form, is conditioned by the redemptive-historical context in which it is given. An easy example is the Sabbath. While the substance of the fourth commandment is universal, the form in which it is given changes (seventh to first day).

But there are other commands God gives that are not universal—for example, the command to destroy the Canaanites. That is a command given to a particular people (Israel) during a particular epoch in redemptive history (Mosaic administration) for a particular purpose (to secure the land for a typological theocracy). More basically, the commands concerning sacrifices are temporary, typological laws given for a time but intended to expire. The same can be said about those laws that are given to Israel as a body politic: Those civil laws are also temporary, with an expiration date.

Therefore, biblicistic preaching falls short of the Great Commission. Any preaching that does not preach Christ from all of Scripture fails to teach disciples to obey all Christ has commanded. Preaching abstractions is to preach Platonic ideals, not the self-attesting Christ of Scripture.

Therefore, our preaching must be systematic. The Great Commission teaching preaches any given passage of Scripture in light of all the other teaching that is found in the record of special revelation. To teach all of what Christ has commanded entails preaching biblical-theologically and systematically.

Preaching Must Be Polemical

One of the more stimulating aspects of missiology is the question of the relation between God and the gods. As Christians called to missions—not just missionaries, but us all—how do we understand the relationship between the God of the Bible and the pagan gods worshipped by unbelievers?

Here we find the cross-section between missiology and apologetics. This issue was central over 100 years ago during the great debates concerning Presbyterian foreign missions. During that time, there was an interesting interplay between evolutionary theories in science, comparative religions in the university, the history of religions school in biblical studies, and the "Rethinking Missions" project. Is the situation really one in which it is God against the gods? Or, is it more like God among the gods? To put it succinctly, is the Christian God the one and only true God, or is he just the apex, the most highly evolved conception of man's religious reflection?

More popularly, is Christianity just one valid expression of religion among a host of others, such that all religions—as the Pope has recently stated—are different, but equally valid, pathways to eternal life? These are the kinds of questions that have been asked by missiologists. A similar, but different, issue arose with the insider movement. Can a missionary, or any believer for that matter, be a secret believer? Can he be a Christian but still practicing the native religion? Can he believe in Christianity in his heart while praying the praises of Allah with his lips?

What these issues have in common is the issue of compromise versus the antithesis. If there is a deep, heart-level antithetical relation between the believer and unbeliever, between Christianity and all other religions, between the God of the Bible and all other gods, then the believer—and the missionary—stands *contra mundum*. If the church is to declare the whole counsel of God, there can be no compromise with unbelief. Which means that the church, as she confronts the gods, must be ready to not only preach the gospel but also to defend the faith, clearly articulating what makes Christianity unique and, furthermore, to explain why other religions are false.

Otherwise, if there is no such heart-level antithesis, and Jesus is just one God among all the other gods, then polemical confrontation of false religions is inappropriate. It would be more appropriate to simply teach the golden rule, spur on humanitarian efforts, give tips for more hygienic living, or practice the religion of unbelievers in the hopes that they will come to like us. But, in fact, teaching the whole counsel of God requires that we be prepared to give a defense for the uniqueness of Christ among the gods.

Conclusion: Teaching *Just Is* the Task of the Church in the Great Commission

R. B. Kuiper says, "The church's task is to teach and preach the Word of God. Whatever else it may properly do is subordinate and subsidiary to that task. This is its supreme task."[3]

---

3. R. B. Kuiper, *The Glorious Body of Christ* (Carlisle, PA: Banner of Truth Trust, 1967), 163.

I have several observations to make from Kuiper's somewhat prescriptive statement.

First, the church's task, according to the Great Commission, is to teach and preach. From this task, she must not waver. There are many good things the church could do. But such things are besides teaching and its subsidiary tasks. The church must resist these things. Contrary to the social gospel, the church is not a humanitarian agency. Its task is not to bring relief to the nations. It is to call the peoples of the nations to come to Christ.

Contrary to activistic forms of Protestantism, the church is not an agency of cultural and political transformation. Whatever good work individual believers do in the world, bringing the Christian worldview to bear upon their work, the church—as the church—does not fulfill its task by making Christian microchips, artwork, or dating apps. As beneficial as those things may be. Such things may be fine for individuals or groups of believers to do. But such things must not be confused with "kingdom work" and must not be taken up by the church as the church. Such things are outside of her competence and commission. What we have here is, indeed, a zero-sum game. The more focused the church is on winning the culture war, it is that much more she loses in doing what she is called to do. The church must not try to be that to which she is not called.

Second, notice the subject matter of the teaching. It is the Word of God. There are many useful things the church could teach. But she must not be distracted from teaching the Word of God and must resist thinking that the church is competent to teach things outside of that which pertains to the gathering and perfecting of the saints.

Third, other tasks of the church are subsidiary. And at that, such tasks are regulated by Scripture. For those tasks—like mercy ministry and the sacraments—point to, or flow from, the Word taught and preached. They serve the central ministry of the church.

Finally, I would like to offer some reflections in terms of application. Any distinction between preaching and teaching is merely phenomenological. Yet, we can think of examples where teaching is not preaching. One example is a seminary setting. The professor is teaching, not preaching, at least in some classes that is more obvious than in others. Yet, many of us have had those professors whose teaching in the classroom often slides back and forth from lecture to sermon. I can think of lectures I sat under from Dick Gaffin, Sinclair Ferguson, and Lane Tipton.

We might also think about a Sunday school class. Certainly, Mrs. Smith's Sunday school class working through Great Commission Publications materials isn't preaching. And the adult Sunday school class going through church history or working through Rosario Butterfield's latest book in no way qualifies as preaching.

So, we perceive that some activities are not preaching but strictly teaching. So, is there a distinction between preaching and teaching such that the Great Commission would be thought of as teaching but not preaching? I do not think so. That is because, I submit to you, seminaries and Sunday school—with all of their importance for the ministry of the church—are not part of the Great Commission itself. In fact, neither are commanded in Scripture. And certainly, such important activities are not in the immediate purview of Jesus when he says, "teaching them to observe all that I have commanded you" (Matt. 28:20a).

So, are these activities excluded? Of course not! All the work of the church is preaching. All the work of the church is teaching. Preaching and teaching *just is* the work of the Great Commission. It is how disciples are made and instructed in what Jesus commanded. But it is not the only activity of the church. There are other para-homiletical activities that the church may do. What is most important, however, when considering in which activities the church should engage, is to ask if such activity either supports the ministry of the Word or flows directly from it.

Take as an example diaconal ministry. This ministry is a para-homiletical activity that supports preaching. But it is also a required activity since it is established as a perpetual office in the church. And we know that because Paul provides for and commends the office to the second post-apostolic generation of ministers through Timothy. Also, the requirement to show mercy to the saints is a ministry provided for in both the Law and the New Testament. Mercy ministry may be para-homiletical, but it is not optional.

What about the sacraments? The sacraments are part and parcel of the Great Commission. That is because they are—as our tradition has emphasized—visible words, or visible Gospels. As such, the sacraments differ from para-homiletical activities. Sacraments are the proclaiming of the gospel but in a different form. In this way, the sacraments are more than merely required (like mercy ministry), but because of their seamless relation to preaching, they are essential. Older works on Reformed polity would say they—along with preaching—are of the *esse* (the being) of the church, not merely of the *bene esse* (well-being) of the church.

What about Mrs. Smith's Sunday school class? This is up for debate, but I see Sunday school as an extension of the parental injunction to raise their children in the fear and admonition of the Lord. It is the church's way to assist parents in their arduous labor to catechize their children. It is not a ministry that replaces the labor of parents but is in support of it. In this way, Sunday school instruction is good, helpful, and useful. It is one possible way for the church to support parents or to supplement preaching in the case of adults. But it is not itself mandated. It is not itself the Great Commission. It is a para-homiletical—that is, optional (not commanded)—and of the *bene esse* of the church.

What about seminary instruction? I might suggest that seminary training, while losing nothing of its academic rigor, should self-consciously become more homiletical. The seminary's teaching should be as devotional as it is academically rigorous. Theological training must be doxological, otherwise it is merely academic. Still, seminary education is para-homiletical. To be sure, it is an indispensable para-homiletical activity. Potential ministers must study to show themselves approved. But the seminary is only one method for doing that. So, while ministers must prepare themselves to rightly handle the word of truth because it is commanded (2 Tim. 2:15), how they are to do so is not commanded. Such preparation, however, is essential to the church's existence and commanded, even if not itself the Great Commission. If ministers need to be prepared to preach the gospel, and the Great Commission *just is* the preaching of the gospel, then such preparation—while para-homiletical—is also quite necessary.

So much more can and should be said. Here I only intend

to offer suggestions on how to apply these things. And perhaps these suggestions will become a topic for later development. But for now, the point is the centrality of preaching and teaching to the Great Commission. It forms the central identity of the church's existence. It is at the core of its nature. And it is the center of the church's work. May God give us grace to stay focused on it, even as we centralize it in our work to carry out the Great Commission.

7

Jesus, the God Who Is with Us to the End of the Age

Matthew 28:20b

Douglas B. Clawson

The Gospel of Matthew begins with a genealogy that emphasizes the descent of Jesus Christ, the anointed one, from Abraham and David. The Gospel concludes with Jesus's declaration that he is with his disciples always, even to the end of the age. Abraham is, humanly speaking, the covenant head of the covenant promising that Abraham's descendants would be his people and that God would be their

God, and David is, humanly speaking, the covenant head of the promise made by God to give his people an eternal king, but it is Jesus alone through whom those covenant promises are kept. He is the one to whom all power and authority is given and whose eternal reign is over all things. He is the one whose disciples, rather than the physical descendants of Jacob, will spread the knowledge of God and the gospel to the ends of the earth. And it is those disciples who, because they are united to him, and his sanctifying Spirit works in them, are made like him through their obedience to all that he commands.

Following the record of three sets of fourteen generations from Abraham to Jesus, Matthew tells us about Mary, who was betrothed to Joseph. She was found to be pregnant but not by Joseph, and just when Joseph would have divorced her quietly, an angel told him not to be afraid because she had conceived by the Holy Spirit and would bear a son called Jesus who would save his people from their sins. Matthew writes: "All this took place to fulfill what the Lord had spoken by the prophet: 'Behold, the virgin shall conceive and bear a son, and they shall call his name Immanuel' (which means, God with us)" (Matt. 1:22–23). It is this name at the beginning of the Gospel—"God with us"—which then is balanced by Jesus's words that close the Gospel—"I am with you always." The meaning of his name, Immanuel, is balanced by his promise to be with his disciples "always, to the end of the age."

The prophesy which Matthew tells us about in 1:22–23 comes from Isaiah 7:14, "Therefore the Lord himself will give you a sign. Behold, the virgin shall conceive and bear a son and shall call his name Immanuel." It is a prophesy given to the unbelieving King Ahaz promising deliverance from the king of

Syria and the empire of Assyria in Isaiah 8.

Like the promise of a child whose name means "God with us" given to an unbelieving king, the child who is the fulfillment of that promise is given to God's people in the days of the unbelieving king Herod, promising not the deliverance of their land from national enemies but promising to save his people from their sins. And it is that Savior, that Immanuel, that "God with us," whose last recorded words in Matthew are "And behold, I am with you always, to the end of the age."

The Nature of God's Presence

When we think about Jesus's promise to be with us to the end of the age, we know that he must be speaking of something other than his omnipresence. He must be speaking of something more than even what Herman Bavinck calls "physical immanence."[1] In the context of Jesus's declaration of having been given all power and authority, and his command to make disciples of all nations, baptizing and teaching them to observe all that he has commanded, the promise of being with them to the end of the age had to have been as intimate and as real as his being there with them on that mountain in Galilee.

The promise of being with them, by necessity, must have been a promise far more than a promise of omnipresence, because there would be no need for the omnipresent God to promise something that is essential to his nature. Nor was it simply a promise of a physical immanence which, as Bavinck points out, God has with every creature since this is the very reason why Paul says to unbelievers: "Yet he is actually not far from each one of us, for 'In him we live and move and have our

---

1. Bavinck, *Reformed Dogmatics*, 2:233.

being'" (Acts 17:27–28). God is physically immanent with every creature. Therefore, if Jesus was promising physical immanence, there would not have been anything especially significant about it. If the promise at the close of Matthew is not a reference to omnipresence or physical immanence, then what is it? What was Jesus promising them? What is Jesus promising us?

Of course, this final promise of Jesus being with his disciples to the end of the age points beyond itself to the consummation of this age and to the next age when the dwelling of God is with man, when he is their God, and they are his people. However, to properly understand that end, it is important for us to look at the promise and realities that lead us to it. Jesus's promise is not as we might initially think—a new and unique promise to those who are in communion with God. It is a promise that is in direct line with what was lost in the fall and with what is fully realized in the new heavens and the new earth. Man didn't only lose original righteousness, holiness, and true knowledge. Most importantly, man lost union and communion with God (WCF 6.2; WLC 27; WSC 19). While part of our lack of appreciation for this loss may be the result of an unclear understanding of what that union and communion was like before the fall or what it will be like in the glorified state, our failure to understand is at least exacerbated by pagan notions of holy space and enlightenment conceptions of time and space.

For example, an enlightenment reading of Genesis 3:8–9, "And they heard the sound of the Lord God walking in the garden in the cool of the day, and the man and his wife hid themselves from the presence of the Lord God among the trees of the garden. But the Lord God called to the man and said to him, 'Where are you?'" almost makes us think of a game of hide-and-seek. Our thinking is bounded by the principle that says two objects cannot occupy the same space. Therefore, God's manifestation in a corporeal-like appearance, or sometimes as the angel of the Lord, can confuse us. God's material-like appearance must not lead us to a view of God that limits him. There is never any place where he is not. There is never any time when he is not near his creatures.

In God's design to make us understand the communion that was lost in the fall into sin, and how he would restore that communion, God portrayed in his tabernacle and his temple a meeting place between God and man. It was a place made holy because it was chosen by God himself to be the place where he would live in the midst of his people. It was a place that was to be kept holy through sacrifices for sin. It pointed his people then and now beyond God living in a confined place to God living with his people and in his people.

God with Us in the Wilderness

Therefore, passages like Exodus 25:8, "And let them make me a sanctuary, that I may dwell in their midst," make our minds think of a holy place where God would confine his living among but separately from his people. Here were their tents, and there was his tent. Even the barriers around the tabernacle and later around the temple reinforced the idea of a no-crossing line, like the barrier that had been around Mount Sinai before God descended from it into the camp in Exodus 40.

But while that may sometimes be the concept that sticks in our minds, I want us to hear the overwhelming number of passages that go beyond that. These passages don't emphasize separation as much as they point us to an intermingling of God with his people in the camp. There wasn't his space and their space but a shared space in which God and his people lived together.

> I will dwell among the people of Israel and will be their God. And they shall know that I am the Lord their God, who brought them out of the land of Egypt that I might dwell among them. I am the Lord their God. (Ex. 29:45–46)

> I will make my dwelling among you, and my soul shall not abhor you. And I will walk among you and will be your God, and you shall be my people. (Lev. 26:11–12)

> The Lord spoke to Moses, saying, "Command the people of Israel that they put out of the camp everyone who is leprous or has a discharge and everyone who is unclean through contact with the dead. You shall put out both male and female, putting them outside the camp, that they may not defile their camp, in the midst of which I dwell." (Num. 5:1–3)

> You shall not pollute the land in which you live, for blood pollutes the land, and no atonement can be made for the land for the blood that is shed in it, except by the blood of the one who shed it. You shall not defile the land in which you live, in the midst of which I dwell, for I the Lord dwell in the midst of the people of Israel. (Num. 35:33–34)

> You shall have a place outside the camp, and you shall go out to it. And you shall have a trowel with your tools, and when you sit down outside, you shall dig a hole with it and turn back and cover up your excrement. Because the Lord your God walks in the midst of your camp, to deliver you and to

give up your enemies before you, therefore your camp must be holy, so that he may not see anything indecent among you and turn away from you. (Deut. 23:12–14)

I know that we tend to want to conceive of the camp as being a holy barrier between the holy tent where God lived and the wilderness outside the camp. But these verses are something more than that.

The demand for the Israelites' holiness wasn't just a barrier; it was essential for the intermingling of God in the camp. The reality of God's presence was so great for Moses that Moses's prayers for God to forgive Israel sometimes contained the element of asking God not to stop living with his people. For example, following the incident of the golden calf, which seemed like a deal breaker to God's continued presence with his people, Moses prayed in Exodus 33:15–16, "And he said to him, 'If your presence will not go with me, do not bring us up from here. For how shall it be known that I have found favor in your sight, I and your people? Is it not in your going with us, so that we are distinct, I and your people, from every other people on the face of the earth?" And in 34:9, he prays: "If now I have found favor in your sight, O Lord, please let the Lord go in the midst of us, for it is a stiff-necked people, and pardon our iniquity and our sin, and take us for your inheritance."

Unlike the pagan concept of a god, that confines a god to a place, such as a sacred grove, tree, spring, shrine, or temple, the Mosaic Law clearly portrays the true God as one who lived in and moved about the camp of Israel, with a view toward God living in the land and moving about in the midst of his people.

Yes, of course, the ark of the covenant, the tabernacle, and later the temple, and the city of Jerusalem came to be the focused symbols of the place of his presence. However, we must remember that they were only symbols. God lived with them, and his presence was seen as so extensive and complete that Moses understood that it wasn't only that God lived among his people, it was also the case that Israel lived with or in the space occupied by God. Moses expresses this in some of his very last words when he says in Deuteronomy 33:27, "The eternal God is your dwelling place, and underneath are the everlasting arms." He expresses this also in his prayer found in Psalm 90:1, "Lord, you have been our dwelling place in all generations. Before the mountains were brought forth, or ever you had formed the earth and the world, from everlasting to everlasting you are God."

Moses understood that God lived with his people, not just separately, but among them. He also understood that God's people lived with God. The cloud and column of fire might stand ahead of or behind them or over them, the tabernacle may have been set up in the middle of the twelve encamped tribes with its courts and its outer and inner holy places, but God was very much present among his people in the camp; he walked where they walked. And God's presence was so extensive and intensive that it wasn't only that he lived among them, it was also that they lived "among" him.

God with Us in the Land

While we can't know what Jesus's words meant to the eleven, we can see that they had a context for understanding them. That context was in the Law, and it was in the Prophets. While the following centuries of revelation would focus on Jerusalem and the temple as the dwelling place of God in the midst of his people, the idea of the intensive and extensive presence of

God with his people was not lost.

God himself encouraged Joshua to have courage when he said, "No man shall be able to stand before you all the days of your life. Just as I was with Moses, so I will be with you. I will not leave you or forsake you" (Josh. 1:5). Was this promise no more special than the way that God is present with every creature? Did this promise require Joshua's close proximity to the tabernacle?

In the chapter of Isaiah just after the prophesy concerning the son conceived and born of a virgin, who shall be called Immanuel, whose name means "God is with us," the word *Immanuel* is used two more times. We read:

> "Therefore, behold, the Lord is bringing up against them the waters of the River, mighty and many, the king of Assyria and all his glory. And it will rise over all its channels and go over all its banks, and it will sweep on into Judah, it will overflow and pass on, reaching even to the neck, and its outspread wings will fill the breadth of your land, O Immanuel." Be broken, you peoples, and be shattered; give ear, all you far countries; strap on your armor and be shattered; strap on your armor and be shattered. Take counsel together, but it will come to nothing; speak a word, but it will not stand, for God is with us. (Isa. 8:7–10)

First, the name "God is with us" is given to the son born of a virgin in Isaiah 7:14, then "Immanuel" is the name given to the land of Israel in Isaiah 8:8, and finally we are told that the attacks of the Assyrians on Judah will fail because "God is with them" in verse 10. Therefore, Immanuel is used as the name of a son, the name of the land, and as a description of God's presence with his people. This combination of ideas expresses what we saw in Moses. God living with his people and his people living with him. This is a concept Isaiah will use once again in verse 14 where we read, "And he will become a sanctuary and a stone of offense and a rock of stumbling to both houses of Israel, a trap and a snare to the inhabitants of Jerusalem." Here we see that the people of God live in him. He is their sanctuary. And his presence is so intense (for a lack of a better word), so present, that he will make them trip over or be trapped by him.

This idea is not only present in the pre-exilic Isaiah; it is also found in the exilic Jeremiah and Ezekiel. Jeremiah writes: "Why should you be like a man confused, like a mighty warrior who cannot save? Yet you, O Lord, are in the midst of us, and we are called by your name; do not leave us" (Jer. 14:9). However, God's leaving his people is the very thing that another exilic prophet tells us that God does. Ezekiel sees the glory of the Lord leave the temple and rest on the east gate of the temple court (Ezek. 10:18–19). After being shown more of the wickedness practiced by the priests and being told the evil things that are said about those in exile, Ezekiel sees God's glory leave the east gate of the temple and leave the city of Jerusalem to rest on the mountain east of the city (Ezek. 11:22–23).

The question might well be asked, If God leaves his people in Jerusalem and the land called by his name, where will he go? That question is answered by some verses in between the movement of God in Ezekiel 10 and the last verses of Ezekiel 11. Speaking of the exiles who are slandered by those in the city, we read in 11:16–17: "Therefore say, 'Thus says the Lord God: Though I removed them far off among the nations, and though I scattered them among the countries, yet I have been a sanctuary to them for a while in the countries where they have gone.' Therefore say, 'Thus says the Lord God: I will gather you from the peoples and assemble you out of the countries where you have been scattered, and I will give you the land of Israel.'" Think of that—God abandons those in the utterly condemned city and condemned land and goes to join and be with his people in their exile! There he becomes their tabernacle, their dwelling place, their tent, the one who covers and protects them and in whom they live.

The post-exilic prophets communicate this as well:

The Lord your God is in your midst, a mighty one who will save; he will rejoice over you with gladness; he will quiet you by his love; he will exult over you with loud singing. (Zeph. 3:17) [This is not the portrayal of a distance between God and his people but of an intimacy reminiscent of a parent holding and singing to his or her child.]

Yet now be strong, O Zerubbabel, declares the Lord. Be strong, O Joshua, son of Jehozadak, the high priest. Be strong, all you people of the land, declares the Lord. Work, for I am with you, declares the Lord of hosts, according to the covenant that I made with you when you came out of Egypt. My Spirit remains in your midst. (Hag. 2:4–5)

... and said to him, "Run, say to that young man, 'Jerusalem shall be inhabited as villages without walls, because of the multitude of people and livestock in it. And I will be to her a wall of fire all around, declares the Lord, and I will be the glory in her midst.'" (Zech. 2:4–5)

Sing and rejoice, O daughter of Zion, for behold, I come and I will dwell in your midst, declares the Lord. And many nations shall join themselves to the Lord in that day, and shall be my people. And I will dwell in your midst, and you shall know that the Lord of hosts has sent me to you. (Zech. 2:10–11)

To be sure, the temple and Jerusalem remain the symbols and focus of God's presence; however, while Jerusalem continues to be the chosen place of God's dwelling and the temple continues to be the chosen place for God's worship, sacrifices, and feasts, the idea of God living outside of those places with his people is not forgotten. It is why Jesus's words in Matthew 28:20b would have been so impactful to the eleven. They may not see him, but he will be just as present. Therefore, when he says, "And behold, I am with you always, to the end of the age," he is saying, "I, Jesus, am the God who will be in your midst. I am sending you to the nations to make disciples, and I will be the one who goes out with you." It is not God as he was known prior to the incarnation, but God as he is known through the revelation of the New Testament who will be with them. It is Jesus who will be with them. Jesus, the God whom they have walked with for three years, will be the one who is with them.

Moses knew by faith the God of Abraham, Isaac, and Jacob who spoke to him at the burning bush; he knew the God who turned his staff into a snake and made his hand leprous; he knew the God who inflicted ten plagues on Pharoah and Egypt and kept him and Israel from lasting harm through all of them; he knew the God who had protected Israel with his cloud and parted the sea; he knew the God who struck down the Amalekites through Israel; he knew the God who spoke at Sinai and met with him for forty days and forty nights on the mountain. He knew by faith that that same God lived extensively and intensively with his people in the camp and would also live with them in the land.

Jesus—God with Us Always and Everywhere

Moses's faith may not have always been appreciated by God's people, but it was a vital part of the fabric of their understanding of the true God. Therefore, here the eleven could know that in the same way, God, Jesus would be with them. They could know by faith that the God who would be with his people as they went out and made disciples is the same Jesus who had called them to be his disciples. The same Jesus changed water into wine, taught and healed, cast out demons, ate in homes, raised the son of a widow and the brother of Martha and Mary. This same Jesus touched lepers and allowed himself to be touched by former prostitutes and a woman unclean because of disease. That same Jesus in front of whom they argued; that same Jesus who rebuked them; that same Jesus who broke bread and poured out wine for them; that same Jesus whom they watched die and whom they now knew to be alive; that same Jesus given all authority in heaven and on earth—is the same Jesus who would be with them extensively and intensively as they went out from everything that they were familiar with into the wilderness of this world to make disciples from all nations. They would never reach a boundary that separated him from them. They would never, ever be alone. Jesus, the Jesus they knew and loved, the Jesus who knew and loved them, would always be with them, everywhere. He would be in them, and they would be in him. It is that same Jesus who is going to be with his disciples always, as he was always with his people in the past. It is the same Jesus who you know through his revelation in the New Testament. The same Jesus who promised to be with them promises to be with you and with all his church to the end of the age.

The Old Testament revelation prepared them, and Jesus prepared them for these words, even when they didn't understand. They had mistakenly thought he would be sitting on a throne reigning in Jerusalem, with one of them on his right and with another on his left. However, he had prepared them for this greater understanding by saying things like the words found in Matthew 18:20: "For where two or three are gathered in my name, there am I among them." And he continues to prepare us for understanding what he means when in Acts 18:9–10, he says to Paul in a vision, "Do not be afraid, but go on speaking and do not be silent, for I am with you, and no one will attack you to harm you, for I have many in this city who are my people." Therefore, he is not a king who sits on a throne in one place, while sending us to another.

How is Jesus with us? He is with us through God's Spirit. We are reminded of this in these passages:

> Do you not know that you are God's temple and that God's Spirit dwells in you? (1 Cor. 3:16)

> What agreement has the temple of God with idols? For we are the temple of the living God; as God said, "I will make my dwelling among them and walk among them, and I will be their God, and they shall be my people." (2 Cor. 6:16)

> So then you are no longer strangers and aliens, but you are fellow citizens with the saints and members of the household of God, built on the foundation of the apostles and proph-

ets, Christ Jesus himself being the cornerstone, in whom the whole structure, being joined together, grows into a holy temple in the Lord. In him you also are being built together into a dwelling place for God by the Spirit. (Eph. 2:19–22)

Jesus is with us always. He is with us, his people, his church, as he moves among us. He is with us as our dwelling place. He is with us as those in whom he lives. He is with us always as we wait for the day when we can say with John in Revelation 21:3–4: "And I heard a loud voice from the throne saying, 'Behold, the dwelling place of God is with man. He will dwell with them, and they will be his people, and God himself will be with them as their God. He will wipe away every tear from their eyes, and death shall be no more, neither shall there be mourning, nor crying, nor pain anymore, for the former things have passed away.'" Just as seeing Jesus is seeing the Father, having the presence of the Spirit is having the presence of Jesus. This presence is his union and communion with us.

Jesus with Us in Union and Communion

Once again, Jesus is neither speaking of his omnipresence nor of what is called his physical immanence that God has with every creature. Rather this is a presence that Jesus has only with those who know him and are known by him. It is an extensive and intensive proximity of relationship summarized in the Westminster Larger Catechism questions and answers that describe our union and communion with God:

> Q. 65. What special benefits do the members of the invisible church enjoy by Christ?

A. The members of the invisible church by Christ enjoy union and communion with him in grace and glory.

Q. 66. What is that union which the elect have with Christ?

A. The union which the elect have with Christ is the work of God's grace, whereby they are spiritually and mystically, yet really and inseparably, joined to Christ as their head and husband; which is done in their effectual calling.

Q. 69. What is the communion in grace which the members of the invisible church have with Christ?

A. The communion in grace which the members of the invisible church have with Christ, is their partaking of the virtue of his mediation, in their justification, adoption, sanctification, and whatever else, in this life, manifests their union with him.

Q. 83. What is the communion in glory with Christ which the members of the invisible church enjoy in this life?

A. The members of the invisible church have communicated to them in this life the firstfruits of glory with Christ, as they are members of him their head, and so in him are interested in that glory which he is fully possessed of; and, as an earnest thereof, enjoy the sense of God's love, peace of conscience, joy in the Holy Ghost, and hope of glory. . . .

I have drawn parallels between what was revealed to Moses for God to be with Israel in the wilderness, and what it meant for the disciples, as Jesus sent them out, to assure them that he would be with them always as they went to the ends of the earth to the end of the age. Jesus would be with and among them. He would be in them by his Holy Spirit, and he would be to them their shelter and place of safety in the wilderness of this world.

Jesus Is the I AM Who Sent Moses into Egypt and He Is the I AM Who Sends Us into the World

So, I would like to leave you with one last thought. In Exodus 3:13 after God gave instructions to Moses that he was to go to Pharoah and to the elders of Israel, "Moses said to God, 'If I come to the people of Israel and say to them, "The God of your fathers has sent me to you," and they ask me, "What is his name?" what shall I say to them?'" God's answer is found in verse 14: "'I am who I am.' . . . 'Say this to the people of Israel: "I am has sent me to you."'" That God is Jesus. We know this to be true because of what we read in John 8:58, "Jesus said to them, 'Truly, truly, I say to you, before Abraham was, I am.'"

In the Greek "I am" is simply Ἐγώ εἰμι. Here in Matthew 28:20, Jesus says "ἐγὼ μεθ' ὑμῶν εἰμι"—"I with you am." The God who promises in Hebrews 13:5 to "never leave or forsake you," is Jesus, the I AM WHO I AM who sent Moses to Pharoah and the elders of Israel to lead Israel out of their slavery through the baptism of the waters of the Red Sea, to be his people, God's disciples, who were taught to observe all that God commanded them in the laws given at Sinai.

Jesus is the I AM WHO I AM who sent Moses. Jesus is the "I with you am" who sends his church. Jesus sent Moses. Jesus sent his apostles. Jesus sends his church to lead those who have been chosen to be his people, to become his disciples, out of their slavery to sin, through baptism, teaching them to observe all that he has commanded.

In your going and making disciples, you are never alone. He will never leave or forsake you. He does not simply send you to the lost in their slavery and their lives in the valley of the shadow of death. Jesus is with you as you go into that dark and condemned wilderness. He is with you and them as together you wait for the eternal day when the dwelling of God is with man. You in him and him in you—"spiritually and mystically, yet really and inseparably" (WLC 66)—Jesus is with you always.

Appendix

Reformed Forum and Global Theological Education

Our Organization

Reformed Forum is committed to providing Reformed Christian theological resources for pastors, scholars, and anyone seeking to deepen their understanding of Scripture and the theology that faithfully summarizes its teachings. Rooted in the principles of the Reformation and a redemptive-historical approach to the Bible, we hold Scripture as the sole standard for faith and life.

Since our founding in January 2008, our vision has been to make the rich theological heritage of the Reformed tradition freely accessible to people around the world. Our flagship program, *Christ the Center*, features weekly discussions with pastors and scholars on a wide range of biblical and theological topics. Beyond this, we produce video courses, organize educational events, publish books, and equip believers with resources for lifelong growth in Christ.

We do not wish to keep these truths to ourselves. Our desire is to see people everywhere grow in their knowledge of God's Word and mature in Christ, sharing in the beauty and depth of Reformed theology as it shapes lives and strengthens the church.

Reformed Forum is incorporated as a non-profit organization in Pennsylvania and recognized by the US Internal Revenue Service as a 501(c)(3) tax-exempt organization (EIN: 27-2306841). Members of our Board of Directors must be members in good standing of churches within the North American Presbyterian and Reformed Council (NAPARC) or the International Council of Reformed Churches (ICRC). These churches subscribe either to the Three Forms of Unity (Canons of Dort, Belgic Confession, and Heidelberg Catechism) or the Westminster Confession of Faith and Catechisms. A majority of our Board of Directors must also be ordained officers.

The Great Commission

> Now the eleven disciples went to Galilee, to the mountain to which Jesus had directed them. And when they saw him they worshiped him, but some doubted. And Jesus came and said to them, "All authority in heaven and on earth has been given to me. Go therefore and make disciples of all nations, baptizing them in the name of the Father and of the Son and of the Holy Spirit, teaching them to observe all that I have

commanded you. And behold, I am with you always, to the end of the age." (Matt. 28:16–20)

Christ entrusted his church with this commission. At Reformed Forum, we believe it is not the purview of parachurch organizations to carry this out properly, which is why we seek to support the church in this mission rather than take it up directly as an organization.

In the original language, there is one imperative in the Great Commission: "make disciples." It is one Greek word: μαθητεύσατε. Everything else qualifies what it means to make disciples. Initially, it involves "going" into the world. This activity is therefore global, and the church must not discriminate among ethnic or socio-economic groups. God has chosen his people from among all nations, and the church must take the message of Christ crucified to the ends of the earth.

This "making" of disciples is further qualified by the activity of baptizing and teaching. Jesus commands the church to baptize them in the name of the Father and of the Son and of the Holy Spirit. Baptism signifies entrance into the covenant community by virtue of union with Christ. Yet disciples must not only be brought into the covenant community, they must also be taught. The content of this instruction is all that Christ has commanded the church. We may say with Paul that it is the "whole counsel of God" (Acts 20:27). In this manner, the church is entrusted with the activity of caring for God's people from grace to glory. It is a lifetime work of discipleship.

The Great Commission is the mission statement of the church. It is what we are about as Christians, and until all of Christ's sheep are brought into his fold, this work must continue. Nevertheless, the church does not engage in this activity on her own. Christ has promised always to be with his people. Indeed, he has sent to them a Helper, the Holy Spirit. Through the Spirit, we are confident that God will complete his work on the day of Jesus Christ (Phil. 1:6).

While the church is entrusted with this singular focus, the ministry of the Great Commission takes different forms in different contexts. If there are established denominations, presbyteries, and local churches, the Great Commission will typically function in the form of Christian Education. If presbyteries and regional church networks exist, but not local churches, Great Commission tasks will function in the form of Home Missions (e.g. church planting). If there is no denomination, it will function as Foreign Missions.

It is important to see that Christian Education, Home Missions, and Foreign Missions are working on the exact same mission. Fundamentally, they are doing the same work: making disciples, baptizing them, and teaching them all that Christ has commanded. But different contexts require different particular emphases until the church grows in that context. These differences are a matter of maturity, which is precisely how Reformed Forum seeks to serve.

Our Mission

Reformed Forum exists to present every person mature in Christ (Col. 1:28).

When Paul spoke of maturity in Colossians 1:28, he used a word (τέλειον) that parallels the emphasis of the Great Commission (discipleship through baptizing and teaching) by indicating initiation into Christ as well as growth (see also Phil. 3:15). Paul likely was co-opting a technical term often used for initiates into Colossian mystery religions, but he certainly had in mind much more than entrance into Christ. Indeed, he sought "to make the word of God fully known" (Col. 1:25).

Ultimately, this is the work of the Holy Spirit working in the church through the means of grace (Word, sacraments, prayer). Reformed Forum is committed to assisting the church in this maturation process. We support the church specifically by encouraging a fidelity to the sufficiency of Scripture in all aspects of the Great Commission. The Reformed tradition generally, and Vos and Van Til specifically, are merely striving to be radically faithful and consistent to Scripture in its fullness.

During the modernist-fundamentalist controversy and Presbyterian conflict of the early twentieth century, E. J. Young wrote to J. Gresham Machen, the founder of Westminster Theological Seminary and key figure in the Orthodox Presbyterian Church, which had yet to be formed:

> Within the church there should be an organization, entirely independent of the formal church, which would act as leaven. This organization should be composed of ministers, elders and laymen of the new church alone, who not only believe the Westminster Confession but who are on fire with it. The purpose of this organization should be to propagate and to defend the Reformed faith, to point out the errors of modernism, sacerdotalism, premillennialism, Arminianism, Trichotomy, and so much of the anti-Scriptural evangelism of today. Furthermore, this group would seek to propagate Reformed literature, such as your book, *Christianity and Liberalism*, Boettner's book and works of that type. It would seek to propagate this literature not only among the clergy

but also among the laity. In other words, it would be a missionary agency whose primary field is the church. Further, it would eventually seek to promote truly Reformed Bible Conferences and Evangelistic Campaigns, would seek to start Reformed Bible classes and prayer meetings and would seek to encourage Reformed radio broadcasts, etc.[1]

Seventy-three years passed before Reformed Forum was founded and much has changed regarding technology, but we believe providentially we have become such an organization. There is a need today just as there was then, because the theological challenges persist. We are committed to be faithful to Scripture to the end that Christ would be glorified in the fulfillment of the Great Commission.

Global Missions

We desire to support the church, not to replace it. Our Lord gave the keys of his kingdom to the church. The church administers the means of grace. Laborers within our organization are members of the church, and in many cases ordained ministers, yet as an organization, Reformed Forum is not the church, nor are we an agency of any particular denomination. Our commitment is to provide resources rooted in Reformed doctrine, along with theological and technological expertise, to churches, denominations, and federations engaged in global missions. We believe the following:

- Theological education is best engaged within a community of believers.

---

1. E. J. Young to J. Gresham Machen, 2 October 1935.

- For healthy indigenous churches to be established and thrive, it is imperative to cultivate long-term discipleship. The effectiveness of theological education is severely hindered through a short-term or drop-in approach.
- Relationships in the mission field in the context of local and regional churches promotes accountability while also encouraging students toward maturity in Christ.

• By his Word and Spirit, Christ instructs and equips his body to operate according to his commands.

- We believe the biblical doctrine of the church (ecclesiology) is summarily comprehended in the historic Reformed creeds and confessions.
- This teaching includes but is not limited to the doctrine of the covenant, church membership, special office, government and polity, and discipline.

As historian of the Orthodox Presbyterian Church (OPC), Rev. Charles Dennison spoke of the denomination in an age when people were seeking to minimize Reformed doctrinal distinctives in favor of emphasizing what they thought were more practical concerns. We believe this message is applicable to all Christians who have come to embrace the richness of the Reformed creeds and confessions.

> The OPC must live on a different plane if she is to be true to the gospel and herself. Her ministry must be practical without becoming "familiar" or pedestrian about the things

of God. She must not be naïve about the theological environment. Her commitment to the Reformed faith must be intelligent and singular; her articulation of it must be unembarrassed and direct. The church must not allow the world either to seduce her or to intimidate her. Above all, she must grasp ever more perfectly the costliness of her devotion to her Savior and be capable of saying with Paul, "God forbid that I should glory, save in the cross of our Lord Jesus Christ, by whom the world is crucified unto me, and I unto the world" (Galatians 6:14).[2]

In our support of the Christ's body, it is imperative that Reformed Forum share this commitment. Particularly in global theological education, our articulation of biblical truth—so well summarized in the Reformed creeds and confessions—must be "intelligent and singular," "unembarrassed and direct," always looking to the Lord for his guidance and strength. To him alone be the glory now and forever.

Principles for Engaging in Foreign Missions

We are committed to the type of confessional Reformed approach to missions described by the Orthodox Presbyterian Church's Committee on Foreign Missions, which distinguishes between fully operational and exploratory fields.[3] With

---

2. Charles G. Dennison, "Some Thoughts about Our Identity," in *History for a Pilgrim People*, ed. Danny E. Olinger and David K. Thompson (Willow Grove, PA: Committee for the Historian of the Orthodox Presbyterian Church, 2002), 206.

3. "Making Disciples of All the Nations: A Plan for Reformed Foreign Missions Orthodox Presbyterian Church," accessed September 12, 2024, https://opc.org/cfm/Making_disciples.html.

regard to the former, the goal is the establishment of a healthy indigenous national church

- that is firmly and fully committed to the Reformed standards;
- that is self-supporting, self-governing, and self-propagating;
- with whom the sending denomination may have fraternal relations;
- that is itself sending out foreign missionaries to other nations; and
- which no longer needs the services of foreign missionaries.

We desire to labor together with any organization that shares our confessional standards and corresponding doctrine of the church particularly as it applies to the carrying out of the Great Commission in foreign fields.

Global Education through Reformed Academy

One of the key ways we support global missions is through Reformed Academy, our educational platform designed to help the church fulfill its mission of presenting every person mature in Christ (Col. 1:28). Reformed Academy offers structured theological education, providing students with opportunities to enroll in courses, watch instructional videos, explore recommended books and articles, complete assessments, and engage with fellow students and faculty. Through this comprehensive learning environment, we aim to equip believers with the knowledge and resources to grow in their faith and service to Christ.

Since launching Reformed Academy in 2020, we have welcomed more than 6,000 students from 90 countries. Through our free, online, on-demand courses, believers around the world are growing in their understanding of Christ crucified and raised for sinners. We currently offer 24 courses, all available at no cost to students, ensuring accessibility to everyone, anytime. Our faculty have outlined 89 future courses across a full range of theological disciplines—including New Testament, Old Testament, systematic theology, church history, and apologetics—catering to various academic levels, from adult Sunday school to advanced MDiv and ThM/PhD studies.

We are also committed to expanding global accessibility by providing foreign language subtitles. Eight courses already feature Spanish and Simplified Chinese subtitles, carefully translated by Reformed native speakers. As we develop this comprehensive curriculum for Christians of all ages and abilities, we will continue to work diligently toward the realization of our vision, as long as we have the support necessary to sustain it.

To continue offering these resources free of charge, we rely on the generous support of individuals like you. Your partnership enables us to expand Reformed Academy, producing new courses, providing foreign language subtitles, and equipping believers worldwide with sound theological education. Will you join us in this mission to present every person mature in Christ? With your help, we can reach even more students around the globe, ensuring the richness of Reformed theology is accessible to all. Please consider supporting Reformed Forum today at reformedforum.org/donate.

Scripture Index

Old Testament

Genesis
1:1 47
1:7 79
1:9 79
1:9–12 80
1:20–25 80
1:22 78
1:28 78
2:3 78
3 32
3:8–9 122–123
3:15 43
6:5–7 79
6:9 80
7:11 79
8:1 79
8:4 13
8:8–12 79
8:17 80
8:20 80
9:12–16 89
9:18 19 14
9:27 14
10:2–5 14
11 15
11:1–9 15
12:1–3 15
12:2–3 64
12:3 .... 32, 72
17:9–14 98
17:11 89
22 13

Exodus
3:13 135
3:14 135
12:13–14 89
14:27–28 81
15:17 82
19–40 13

147

19:4–6 82
20:1–17 110
25:8 123
28:40 85
29:4 .... 84, 85
29:5–9 85
29:10–20 84
29:12 84
29:20 84
29:28 84
29:32–33 84
29:45–46 124
31:16–17 89
33:15–16 125
34:9 125
40 123

Leviticus
8 84
8:6 85
26:11–12 124

Numbers
1–10 13
5:1–3 124
8:5–7 .... 85n9
35:33–34 124

Deuteronomy
5:6–21 110
23:12–14 124–125
33:27 126

Joshua
1:5 127

1 Kings
11:36 13
14:21 13

2 Kings
21:4 13

Psalms
89:4 45
89:36–37 45–46
90:1 126

Isaiah
2 21
2:1–4 72
2:2–4 12
2:3 18
7:14 .... 120, 127
8   121
8:7–10 127
8:8 127
8:10 127
8:14 128
11:9 .... 17, 22
40:4 13
42:6–7 16

44:3 92
49:6 16
51:9–10 81
52:10 62
54:2–3 .... 10n5
57:15 58–59
60:1–3 16
61 18

Jeremiah
4:4 98
14:9 128
31:36 92

Ezekiel
10:18–19 128
11:16–17 128–129
11:22–23 128
28:13–15 13

Daniel
2:44–45 45–46
7:13 49

Hosea
14:8 93

Jonah
2:9 89

Micah
4:1–5 72

Habakkuk
2:4 34

Zephaniah
3:17 129

Haggai
2:4–5 129

Zechariah
2:4–5 129
2:10–11 130
6:13 41

NEW TESTAMENT

Matthew 46–47
1:22–23 120
7:21–23 .... 90, 92
11:27 89
12:41 89
16:18–19 96
18:20 132
19:13–14 92
24:37 81
25:31–46 90

26:64 49
28:16–20 139
28:18 .... 37–59, 38, 48, 50, 57, 61
28:18–20 .... 11, 37–38, 76, 108
28:19a 61–73, 61, 61–62, 66–68
28:19b 75–99, 76
28:19–20 .... 38, 62
28:20 .... 38, 50, 57, 102, 106, 107, 108, 120, 122, 135
28:20a 101–117, 104, 115
28:20b 119–136, 130

Mark 46–47
6:9–20 107
10:13 97
14:62 49
16:15 107–108

Luke 46–47
1:33 45–46
3:8 95
3:16 90
4:16–30 18
9:23 55
12:50 87
18:15 95

18:16 95
24:27 108
24:46–49 104
24:47 104–105

John
3:36 90
4:1–2 .... 90n16
4:35 62
5:21–24 89
6:36 .... 90n16
8:58 135
10:16 106
15:5 93
15:8 95
16:8 88
21:15–19 105–107

Acts
1–2 104–105
1:8 .... 19, 104–105
2 .... 19, 105
2:32–33 .... 50, 50–51
2:33 50
2:39 .... 92, 96
2:42 25–26
6:2–4 26
6:7 26
9:15 30
11:18 93
15 20

17:27–28 122
17:31 90
18:9–10 132
20:27 .... 67, 139
28:31 105

Romans 33
1:1–7 26
1:8 27
1:8–10 26
1:8–17 .... 25–36, 26
1:9 27
1:10 28
1:11 .... 28, 34
1:11–12 26
1:13 30
1:13–15 26
1:14 30
1:15 .... 29, 31
1:16 .... 31, 32
1:16–17 26
1:17 33
3:26 33
6:3 87
6:3–4 82
6:4 87
6:17 102
6:17–23 82
8:4 .... 91, 93
8:9 58
8:9b 50
8:10 58
8:17 55
9–11 20
10 32
10:9 33
19:17 93
11:11–24 20
15:24 30
15:28 30
16:25 33

1 Corinthians
3:16 132
7:14 .... 92, 97
10:2 83
10:3–4a 83
10:4b 83
12:6 93
15:10 93
15:24 .... 53, 80
15:28 53
15:47 55
15:58 .... 59, 72

2 Corinthians
1:20 17
4:10 55
4:13 95
5:10 90
5:17 80
6:16 132

Galatians
3:16................64
3:16–29.........18
4:4..................17
5:16................91
6:14................144

Ephesians
1:20................48
1:22................51
1:22–23.........49–50
2:6..................55
2:8–9 93
2:11–15.........13
2:14–16.........65
2:18................89
2:19–22.........133
3:6..................20
3:16–17.........58
4:3..................98
6:1..................92, 97
6:4..................91, 97

Philippians
1:6..................140
2:13................93
3:10................55

Colossians
1:25................141
1:28................102, 109, 140, 145

1:28–29.........68–70, 70–71
3:3..................55, 91
3:16................102

1 Thessalonians
2:11................97
4:17................56

2 Thessalonians
1:11................93

1 Timothy
2:7..................106
4:13................102
4:16................102
5:17................106–107
6:3..................102

2 Timothy
1:11................106
2:15................116
2:25................93
4:2..................25, 107

Hebrews
6:20................55
10:19 85–86
10:22 86
12:22 55
12:22–24.......21
13:5................135
13:21 93

1 Peter

1:2	97
1:11	50
2:4–5	85
2:9	82
3:6–7	81
3:10	81
3:18	89
3:20–21a	80–81

2 Peter

3:6–7	79

Revelation

6:16	91
7:9	20, 65
7:9–10	72
15:3	82
20:14–15	92
21:3–4	133
22:1	78

Made in the USA
Columbia, SC
31 March 2025